MASTERCHEF
GOES LARGE

MASTERCHEF
GOES LARGE

Become an Expert Chef in Your Own Kitchen

EBURY
PRESS

NOTE: All recipes serve 4 unless otherwise stated

This book is based on the television series *Masterchef Goes Large*, produced
for the BBC by Shine Limited in association with Ziji Productions Limited in 2005 and 2006.

Series editor: John Silver
Series producer: Karen Ross
Executive producers: Elisabeth Murdoch and Franc Roddam
BBC Head of Factual Commissioning, Independents: Jo Clinton-Davis
BBC Senior Commissioning Executive, Daytime: Dominic Vallely

Introduction © Thomasina Miers 2005
John Torode's masterclasses, tips and recipe introductions © John Torode 2005
Recipes and all other copy © Shine Limited 2005
Photography © Brent Darby 2005, except pages 2–3, 5, 10–11, 28, 37, 44–5, 48,
76–7, 103, 112–13, 145, 150 and 159 © Mark Read 2005, and page 6
© Richard Learoyd 2005.

John Torode has asserted his right to be identified as the author of his
masterclasses and other contribution in accordance with the Copyright, Design
and Patents Act 1988.

By arrangement with the BBC.
The BBC logo is a trade mark of the British Broadcasting Corporation
and is used under licence.
BBC logo © BBC 1996

First published in the United Kingdom in 2005 by
Ebury Press, 1 Stephen Street, London W1T 1AL

This paperback edition published 2006.

Random House Australia (Pty) Limited
20 Alfred Street, Milsons Point, Sydney, New South Wales 2061, Australia

Random House New Zealand Limited
18 Poland Road, Glenfield, Auckland 10, New Zealand

Random House South Africa (Pty) Limited
Isle of Houghton, Corner Boundary Road & Carse O'Gowrie, Houghton 2198, South Africa

Random House UK Limited Reg. No. 954009
www.randomhouse.co.uk

Design: Smith & Gilmour, London
Copy editor: Jane Middleton
Editorial consultant: Samantha Scott-Jeffries
Photography: Brent Darby, Mark Read and Richard Learoyd
Food stylist: Louise Mackaness
Props stylist: Harriet Docker
Home economist: Ita Nugent
Legal executives for Shine Limited: Rachel House and John Villeneuve

A CIP catalogue record for this book is available from the British Library.

Papers used by Ebury Press are natural, recyclable products
made from wood grown in sustainable forests.

ISBN: 0091910897 (ISBN-13: 9780091910891 from January 2007)

Printed and bound by Appl Druck Wemding, Germany

With thanks to: Westminster College, Smiths of Smithfield, Vernon Mascarenhas,
Stan Gwilliam, Faye Stewart, Lynsey Kent, Kirsten Bartlett, Louise Penoz,
Martine Carter, Rosemary Scoular, Paul Stevens, Fiona Macintyre, Carey Smith,
Sarah Lavelle, Katherine Hinckley and Jim, Emma, Alex, Keith and Saskia at
Smith & Gilmour, London.

CONTENTS

Introduction

by Thomasina Miers, Masterchef 2005

'Winning Masterchef will change your life...'

That phrase, heard at the start of each programme, reverberated around my head for six weeks as I compulsively watched the series on television at home, having bust a gut filming it three months earlier. I would finally find out what Gregg Wallace, John Torode and the other judges had really said about me and my cooking during the various hair-raising challenges I had faced – on board a ship, cooking over fire pits for the army, feeding pop stars the Corrs at Wembley, making a soufflé for Michel Roux... The first time I saw myself on television it felt very strange; seeing myself with my emotions bared to the world brought tears to my eyes.

Being on *Masterchef Goes Large* mixed intense, high-octane adrenaline when cooking with nervous angst while waiting to hear what people thought about the food. During the filming I ate, slept and dreamt food for weeks on end. My head was never out of at least four different books: I fell asleep over cookbooks, woke up over cookbooks and muttered food combinations and recipes to myself as I cycled to the studio every morning. I learnt more about seasonal food than ever before and intensified my quest for fresh ingredients, local produce and simple cooking. *Masterchef* not only taught me my strengths and weaknesses in the kitchen but also made me more fascinated by food than I had ever been before. I discovered that I really was passionate about food (my friends had been trying to tell me this for years), which in itself was a big step forward. Having spent years convincing myself that I shouldn't become a chef, all those doubts went by the wayside.

After winning *Masterchef*, and thanks to the encouragement of John and Gregg, I found a job cooking at Petersham Nurseries in Richmond, under the careful eye of Skye Gyngell. She is an incredible chef who has an extraordinary ability to turn complex blends of spices and herbs into the simplest, most delicious of dishes. Skye's cooking is focused wholly on the seasons, an approach that I revel in. She has a walled kitchen garden attached to the restaurant, providing a myriad of seasonal produce, from globe artichokes and flowering thyme to courgette flowers and autumnal quince. Cooking there has been a marvellous experience: racing to work over the river and through meadows, prepping like mad for service, fiendishly trying to feed an increasing number of customers every day, creating new dishes, learning about flavours and even doing the occasional mushroom forage. It is hard to believe that only half an hour from my London flat you can seem so immersed in the countryside.

Additionally, my passion for Mexico and its rich range of foods, which was sparked during my gap year, has been focused and helped enormously by winning *Masterchef*. I have since returned to Mexico City, interviewing chefs in order to write articles, cooking with them and developing ideas and new recipes. I even went to New York to work with a fabulous woman, a Mexican chef in an outstanding restaurant there. People seem enthused by my passion for Mexican food. I have done food demonstrations on chillies and chocolate and mastered my stage nerves so as not to slice off my fingers, as I did the first few times!

I have also worked furiously hard on finishing a book, *Soup Kitchen* (www.soupkitchen.org.uk), in which a friend and I collected soup recipes from over a hundred well-known chefs, generously donated by them to raise money for homeless charities across the UK. I have since started work on my own cookbook, which yet again would not have been possible without *Masterchef*.

In this book to tie in with the series, you'll find quite a few of the recipes that I came up with during the competition, including my tasty flash-baked mackerel with beetroot tzatsiki and an autumnal warm salad of partridge breast. And as well as inspired recipes from many of the contestants who took part, there are some invaluable masterclasses from John Torode and a handy list of suppliers from Gregg Wallace.

So I have to admit it, winning *Masterchef* really has changed my life, just as they said it would. Apart from anything else my twin now only ever calls me 'MC' (with a ridiculous, teasing grin on his face!) and I got away without washing up at my parents for at least the first three months afterwards. I am sure it will soon be changing the next winner's life too. Having gone through the inevitable emotional rollercoaster involved in getting to the final, I think he or she will deserve it!

Inspired by contestant Jonathan Grant

Roast Tomato and Red Pepper Soup with Chorizo and Borlotti Beans

The name of this recipe does not do it justice. This is one of those fantastic dishes that you don't except much from initially as it is only a soup, but it gives a massive delivery. The depth of flavour from the chorizo is the main reason for its success. The beans give a great texture and a solid base to what is a wonderful Sunday-evening soup.

→ 400G (14OZ) TOMATOES, CUT INTO QUARTERS
→ 2 RED PEPPERS, CUT INTO LARGE CHUNKS
→ 5 TBSP OLIVE OIL
→ 75G (3OZ) CHORIZO SAUSAGE, CUT INTO SLICES 5MM (1/4 IN) THICK
→ 2 LARGE GARLIC CLOVES, FINELY CHOPPED
→ 1 RED CHILLI, FINELY CHOPPED
→ 400G (14OZ) TIN OF BORLOTTI BEANS, DRAINED AND RINSED
→ 500ML (18FL OZ) HOT VEGETABLE STOCK
→ 4 THICK SLICES OF CIABATTA BREAD
→ SALT AND FRESHLY GROUND BLACK PEPPER

1 Preheat the oven to 200°C/400°F/Gas Mark 6.

2 Put the tomatoes and red peppers in a roasting tin. Season with salt and pepper and toss with 3 tablespoons of the olive oil. Roast for 30–40 minutes, until browned around the edges.

3 Meanwhile, heat the remaining olive oil in a frying pan and gently fry the chorizo in it for 3 minutes. Stir in the garlic and chilli and cook for 2 minutes longer. Remove from the heat and stir in the beans, then set aside.

4 Remove the roasted vegetables from the oven and put them into a blender or food processor with half the vegetable stock. Purée until almost smooth.

5 Pour the mixture into a large saucepan. Add the remaining stock and the chorizo and bean mixture and simmer for 5 minutes.

6 Toast the bread. Divide the soup between 4 bowls and serve with the toast.

'What does it take to make a star chef? Ability, charisma, stamina, food knowledge and most of all, passion.'
John Torode, Masterchef Judge

Cauliflower Soup

Cauliflower soup is an old-fashioned favourite that deserves a revival. The classic cauliflower soup is called crème du Barry, and is said to be named after the comtesse du Barry, a favourite mistress of Louis XV of France.

- → 100G (4OZ) BUTTER
- → 1 ONION, FINELY CHOPPED
- → 1 CELERY STICK, CHOPPED
- → 2 POTATOES, PEELED AND FINELY DICED
- → 450G (1LB) CAULIFLOWER, DIVIDED INTO FLORETS
- → 250G (9OZ) PARSNIPS, FINELY DICED
- → 500ML (18FL OZ) CHICKEN OR VEGETABLE STOCK
- → 250ML (8FL OZ) MILK
- → A FEW SPRIGS OF THYME
- → 2 BAY LEAVES
- → 60ML (2FL OZ) DRY VERMOUTH
- → 100ML (3½FL OZ) DOUBLE CREAM
- → 4 QUAIL'S EGGS
- → A GOOD PINCH OF CAYENNE PEPPER
- → 1 TBSP SNIPPED CHIVES
- → SALT AND WHITE PEPPER

1 Melt the butter in a large saucepan, add all the vegetables, then cover and sweat for 6–7 minutes, until soft but not coloured.

2 Add the stock, milk, thyme and bay leaves. Bring to the boil, then reduce the heat, cover and simmer for 20 minutes. Remove the bay leaves.

3 Purée the soup until smooth and season to taste. Add the vermouth and double cream and reheat the soup, but don't let it boil.

4 Poach the quail's eggs (see tip below) until they are cooked but still soft in the centre. Remove with a slotted spoon and drain on kitchen paper.

5 Ladle the soup into 4 warm bowls. Carefully place a poached quail's egg in each bowl. Sprinkle with a little cayenne pepper and the snipped chives and serve immediately.

MASTERCHEF TOP TIP

To poach quail's eggs, place a pan of water over a high heat and bring to a simmer. Pour 100ml (3½fl oz) white wine vinegar into a cup, then break 4 quail's eggs into it. Pour the eggs and vinegar into the water – the eggs will separate from each other. Leave for 2 minutes, then remove from the water with a slotted spoon and drain on kitchen paper. The eggs will be perfectly cooked.

John Torode, Masterchef Judge

'I don't think you're trying to win Masterchef – you're aiming for your first Michelin star!'

Gregg Wallace, Masterchef Judge, to James Cross

Inspired by contestant Fabian Petitcolas

Butternut Squash Soup with Poppy Seed Cream

This simple little soup is completely uplifted by the addition of a poppy seed cream that sits neatly in the centre. The trick is not to have the bowls too hot or the cream will melt. The little croûtons are also known as sippets and are classically served as an accompaniment to dainty soups such as this one.

→ 400G (14OZ) BUTTERNUT SQUASH, PEELED, DESEEDED AND CUT INTO CHUNKS
→ 200ML (7FL OZ) CHICKEN STOCK
→ 40G (1½OZ) BUTTER
→ LEMON JUICE, TO TASTE
→ A DASH OF TABASCO SAUCE
→ 5 TBSP WHIPPING CREAM
→ 2 TSP POPPY SEEDS
→ 1 TBSP OLIVE OIL
→ 3 SLICES OF WHITE BREAD, CUT INTO 5MM–1CM (¼–½ IN) CUBES
→ SALT AND WHITE PEPPER

1 Put the squash into a large saucepan and add the chicken stock, 25g (1oz) of the butter and 200ml (7fl oz) water. Bring to the boil, then reduce the heat and simmer until the squash is tender.

2 Blend until smooth, adding more water if the soup is too thick. Season with lemon juice, Tabasco and some salt and pepper.

3 Whip the cream and poppy seeds together until thick, then set aside.

4 Melt the remaining butter in a large frying pan with the oil. Add the bread cubes and fry over a high heat until crisp and golden all over. Set aside.

5 Reheat the soup to just simmering; do not let it boil. Pour it into 4 soup bowls and carefully place a tablespoon of the poppy seed cream in the centre of each one. Serve immediately, accompanied by the bread croûtons.

Inspired by contestant Vivian Pei

Rich Cream of Fennel Soup with Crab and Red Pepper Coulis

Originally this soup-come-sauce was presented in martini glasses – pretty but not very practical. It would be wise to serve this very rich soup in small quantities, perhaps as a pre-dinner treat. Although there is a lot of work involved, it is well worth it.

→ 15G (½OZ) BUTTER
→ 1 GARLIC CLOVE, CHOPPED
→ 1 FENNEL BULB, FINELY SLICED
→ 1 LEEK (WHITE PART ONLY), FINELY SLICED
→ 1 FLOURY POTATO, SUCH AS MARIS PIPER, PEELED AND DICED
→ 1 BAY LEAF
→ ABOUT 175ML (6FL OZ) CHICKEN OR VEGETABLE STOCK
→ 1 TSP PERNOD (OPTIONAL)
→ 3 TBSP DOUBLE CREAM
→ 50G (2OZ) FRESH CRAB MEAT (A MIXTURE OF WHITE AND BROWN)
→ SALT AND WHITE PEPPER
→ SPRIGS OF DILL, TO GARNISH
For the red pepper coulis:
→ 15G (½OZ) BUTTER
→ 1 RED PEPPER, CHOPPED
→ 2 TBSP DOUBLE CREAM
→ 1 TBSP TOMATO PURÉE
→ A PINCH OF CAYENNE PEPPER

1 Melt the butter in a saucepan, add the garlic, fennel and leek, then cover and sweat until soft and translucent.

2 Add the potato and bay leaf and pour in enough stock just to cover the vegetables. Cover and simmer for 15–20 minutes, until all the vegetables are tender.

3 Remove the bay leaf and purée the soup until smooth. Pour through a sieve into a clean saucepan and reheat. Stir in the Pernod, if using, and the cream, then season to taste. Cover and keep warm.

4 For the coulis, melt the butter in a small saucepan, add the red pepper and cook over a low heat for 2 minutes. Stir in the cream and tomato purée and season with salt, pepper and the cayenne. Cook over a medium heat for about 10 minutes, stirring occasionally, until the pepper is soft.

5 Purée the mixture in a food processor or liquidiser, then pass it through a sieve into a clean pan. Reheat gently.

6 Spoon a good tablespoon or two of the coulis into 4 glass, ramekin-sized dishes, about 200ml (7fl oz) in capacity. Sprinkle the crab meat over the coulis, then gently spoon the fennel soup over the crab so as not to disturb the layers. Garnish with a sprig of dill. Eat with a teaspoon, scooping through all the layers at once.

Jerusalem Artichoke Soup with White Truffle Oil and Brown Soda Bread Scones

The Jerusalem artichoke is a small, bulbous vegetable with a nutty flavour. It is best cooked simply and this recipe does just that. The soup has a wonderfully rich, velvety texture. Any bread recipe that doesn't require kneading and proving is a good thing, so even if the soup doesn't make it to your table you should try to make the bread regularly. Serve it hot, with lashings of salted butter.

→ 675G (1½LB) JERUSALEM ARTICHOKES
→ A GOOD KNOB OF BUTTER
→ 1 ONION, FINELY CHOPPED
→ 1 POTATO, PEELED AND DICED
→ 750ML (1¼ PINTS) VEGETABLE STOCK
→ 100ML (3½FL OZ) DOUBLE CREAM
→ 2 TBSP WHITE TRUFFLE OIL
→ 2 TBSP CHIVES, SNIPPED
→ SALT AND WHITE PEPPER
   For the soda bread scones:
→ 275G (10OZ) WHOLEMEAL FLOUR
→ 275G (10OZ) PLAIN WHITE FLOUR
→ 1 TSP SALT
→ 1 TSP BICARBONATE OF SODA
→ 400–500ML (14–18FL OZ) BUTTERMILK

1 Preheat the oven to 200°C/400°F/Gas Mark 6.

2 For the scones, mix all the dry ingredients together in a large bowl. Make a well in the centre and add the smaller quantity of buttermilk. Mix by hand, adding more buttermilk if necessary, until you have a soft but not sticky dough.

3 Turn out on to a floured surface and knead lightly – just enough to shape the dough into a round. Flatten it to about 2.5cm (1 in) thick and cut out 8–10 scones, using a 7.5cm (3 in) plain cutter. Put on to a floured baking tray and bake for about 20 minutes, until well risen and golden. Leave to cool on a wire rack.

4 To make the soup, put the unpeeled artichokes in a pan of salted water and bring to the boil. Reduce the heat and simmer for 8 minutes, then drain.

5 Melt the butter in a large saucepan and add the onion and potato. Cover and sweat until soft but not coloured.

6 Peel and mash the artichokes, then stir them into the onion and potato mixture. Add the stock, bring to the boil, then reduce the heat and simmer for 20 minutes.

7 Purée the soup in a blender, then pour through a sieve into a clean pan. Stir in the cream and reheat the soup gently, without letting it boil. Taste and adjust the seasoning.

8 Ladle the soup into 4 warm bowls. Drizzle the truffle oil over the surface and sprinkle with the chopped chives. Serve with the scones.

Inspired by contestant Peter Gerald

Gazpacho with Savoury Cheese Scones

Gazpacho means 'soaked bread', and this is what this soup is all about – a good bread base with punchy, well-seasoned tomatoes and peppers. Serve Tabasco sauce on the side for those who want some extra heat. The crushed ice is a must, as this soup should be served very cold on a hot day.

→ 4 LARGE, SWEET RED TOMATOES, CHOPPED
→ ½ LARGE CUCUMBER, PEELED AND CHOPPED
→ 1 GREEN PEPPER, CHOPPED
→ 150G (5OZ) SPANISH ONION, CHOPPED
→ 1 MILD LONG RED CHILLI, CHOPPED
→ 1 GARLIC CLOVE, FINELY CHOPPED
→ 2 TBSP GOOD-QUALITY WHITE WINE VINEGAR
→ 75G (3OZ) FRESH WHITE BREAD, CRUSTS REMOVED
→ 500ML (18FL OZ) TOMATO JUICE
→ 1 TSP SUGAR
→ SALT AND FRESHLY GROUND BLACK PEPPER

For the scones:
→ 225G (8OZ) SELF-RAISING FLOUR
→ 1 TSP BAKING POWDER
→ A PINCH OF SALT
→ 40G (1½OZ) BUTTER, DICED
→ 50G (2OZ) GRUYÈRE CHEESE, GRATED
→ 50G (2OZ) SUN-BLUSH TOMATOES IN OIL, DRAINED AND CHOPPED
→ 1 EGG
→ 100ML (3½FL OZ) ICE-COLD MILK

To garnish:
→ 4–6 TBSP CRUSHED ICE
→ 4 TBSP EXTRA VIRGIN OLIVE OIL
→ 8 LARGE BASIL LEAVES, SHREDDED
→ TABASCO SAUCE (OPTIONAL)

1 Purée the vegetables, chilli and garlic together in a food processor. Add the vinegar, bread, tomato juice and sugar and process again until thick and smooth. Season to taste, then leave in the fridge until very cold.

2 Put the soup through a fine sieve, pushing the mixture through with the back of a large wooden spoon. Discard any remaining pulp. Chill the soup again.

3 Meanwhile, make the scones. Preheat the oven to 190°C/375°F/Gas Mark 5. Sift the flour, baking powder and salt into a large bowl, then rub in the butter until the mixture resembles fine breadcrumbs. Stir in the grated cheese and tomatoes.

4 Lightly whisk the egg and milk together and pour about three-quarters of this mixture into the flour mixture. Quickly and lightly bind all the ingredients together with a large knife, adding the extra egg mixture if necessary to give a soft, but not sticky, dough. Do not overwork the dough or the scones will be heavy.

5 Tip the dough on to a floured work surface and, working lightly and quickly, shape it into a round about 2.5cm (1 in) deep. Cut out about 8 scones, using a 5cm (2 in) fluted or plain cutter. Brush the tops with a little of the leftover egg mixture.

6 Put the scones on a baking tray lined with baking parchment and bake for 15–18 minutes, until well risen and golden brown.

7 Just before serving, remove the soup from the fridge and taste and adjust the seasoning if necessary. Serve in large bowls with a little crushed ice stirred through, depending on how thick you like your gazpacho. Garnish with the olive oil and basil and sprinkle on a couple of drops of Tabasco, if liked. Serve with the warm scones.

Masterchef Masterclass
John Torode's Hollandaise

Hollandaise is one of the great classic sauces. Once you have mastered it you will be able to make any number of variations, including béarnaise (see page 108). A luxurious emulsion of butter and egg yolks flavoured with lemon juice, hollandaise has a reputation for being difficult because of its tendency to separate. However, as long as you don't overheat it, it should be quite safe. The method opposite may seem long and complicated but it's really worth doing. With a little practice, the whole process should take no longer than fifteen minutes, and it helps to build up your muscles!

Traditionally hollandaise is served warm as an accompaniment to vegetables, fish or eggs. It doesn't keep well, so is best made at the last minute. However, you can keep it warm for up to half an hour if necessary by placing the bowl in a large bowl of warm water or by pouring the sauce into a Thermos flask.

Here are the main points to remember when making hollandaise sauce:

→ For the best flavour, use good-quality, fresh unsalted butter.

→ Whisk the egg yolks thoroughly with the vinegar reduction so that the mixture becomes thick and creamy. This helps to stabilise the mixture once you start adding the butter, so the sauce is less likely to separate.

→ Add the butter very slowly at first, then once the mixture has thickened you can speed it up a little.

→ Never overheat hollandaise. The temperature should not exceed 66°C/150°F.

→ If, despite your best efforts, it does look as if it's about to separate, quickly whisk in a tablespoon of hot water. If this doesn't work, you can start again by repeating steps 1 and 2 opposite and gradually whisking in the curdled mixture (you will have a very rich sauce!).

John Torode's
Basic Hollandaise Sauce

SERVES 6

→ 6 TBSP WHITE WINE
→ 6 TBSP WHITE WINE VINEGAR
→ 20 BLACK PEPPERCORNS
→ 2 BAY LEAVES
→ 3 EGG YOLKS
→ 300G (11OZ) WARM MELTED BUTTER
→ A PINCH OF SALT
→ JUICE OF ½ LEMON

1 Put the white wine and vinegar into a small pan with the peppercorns and bay leaves. Bring to the boil and simmer until reduced to about 3 tablespoons. Leave to cool, then remove the peppercorns and bay leaves.

2 Put the egg yolks into a large, heatproof glass bowl and place it over a pan of barely simmering water, making sure the water isn't touching the base of the bowl. Whisk in about a tablespoon of the vinegar reduction and continue to whisk for 2–3 minutes, until the mixture turns pale and thick and the whisk leaves a trail on the surface when lifted (this is known as the ribbon stage).

3 Remove the bowl from the heat and put it on a folded cloth (to stop it slipping and to keep the heat in) on a work surface. Little by little, whisk in the melted butter, making sure each addition is completely incorporated before adding any more. Keep going until all the butter has been used up and the sauce is thick and creamy. Have a bowl of hot water handy so that you can add a tablespoon if you feel that the sauce might be about to scramble.

4 The finished hollandaise should be a light, pourable consistency. Beat in the salt and lemon juice to taste, then serve.

John Torode's Asparagus with Hollandaise Sauce

SERVES 6
→ 60 ASPARAGUS SPEARS
→ 1 QUANTITY OF HOLLANDAISE
  SAUCE (SEE PAGE 21)
→ SALT

If you want to talk classic, here we are. Like tomato and basil or strawberries and cream, asparagus and hollandaise were made for each other. Buy the freshest possible asparagus, preferably English, which is in season in May and June, and cook it on the same day.

1 The spears have a tough base and a tender stem and tip. Towards the base, where the green starts to turn to white, they will snap naturally. Break each one individually and discard the bases (or save them to make soup). Use twine to tie the asparagus in bundles of 12 or thereabouts. Don't tie them too tight or you will damage them.

2 Make the hollandaise sauce as described on page 21 and keep warm.

3 Fill a large pot with cold water (or a small amount of water in an asparagus steamer, if you have one) and bring to the boil. Add a good teaspoon of salt, then drop in the asparagus bundles. Return to the boil and start checking whether it's tender after 2 minutes.

4 Remove the asparagus from the pan, cut the twine from each bundle and trim the ends of the spears so they are an even length. Drain very thoroughly, then divide between 6 large, warm serving plates and serve straight away, with the hollandaise sauce.

Asparagus, Pancetta and Toasted Ciabatta

When Tony cooked this, he had a few problems with his poached egg (see the masterclass on page 132 for advice) but otherwise he should have been writing a bloke's 'impress-the-girls' cookbook. Simple and clever, this posh open sandwich would benefit from a big blob of garlic mayonnaise (see page 118) or some Caesar salad dressing. The ciabatta could be replaced by any other good bread, such as a pain de campagne or a baguette.

→ 8 SLICES OF PANCETTA
→ 4 THICK SLICES OF CIABATTA BREAD, CUT ON THE DIAGONAL
→ 4 LARGE EGGS
→ 8 LARGE ASPARAGUS SPEARS
→ A SMALL BLOCK OF PARMESAN CHEESE
→ 2 TBSP EXTRA VIRGIN OLIVE OIL
→ 3 LARGE HANDFULS OF ROCKET
→ SEA SALT AND FRESHLY GROUND BLACK PEPPER

1 Preheat the oven to 200°C/400°F/Gas Mark 6. Put 2 large saucepans of salted water on to boil.

2 Lay 2 slices of pancetta on top of each slice of ciabatta bread, place on a baking tray and bake for 5 minutes, until both the ciabatta and the pancetta are crisp.

3 Meanwhile, poach the eggs in one saucepan (see page 132) and boil the asparagus in the other for about 2–3 minutes, until just tender, then drain well (see page 22).

4 Place 2 asparagus spears on top of the pancetta. With a potato peeler, shave a little Parmesan over, then drizzle with the olive oil. Top with a poached egg, some rocket and seasoning, and finally some more Parmesan shavings. Serve immediately.

Inspired by contestant Katherine Haworth

Baked Figs with Ribblesdale Goat's Cheese and Pink Peppercorns

Some people may be surprised by this recipe but, funnily enough, it works. The goat's cheese makes a good contrast to the sweetness of the figs and the sauce.

→ 8 FRESH FIGS
→ 6 TBSP CLEAR HONEY
→ 4 THICK SLICES OF BRIOCHE
→ 1 TBSP PINK PEPPERCORNS, CRUSHED
→ 50G (2OZ) RIBBLESDALE GOAT'S CHEESE, THINLY SLICED
→ A SMALL BUNCH OF CHIVES, FINELY SNIPPED
→ 4 TBSP PLAIN YOGHURT

MASTERCHEF TOP TIP

I don't understand why people go for French goat's cheeses when there are so many good British ones around now. Ribblesdale is an excellent cheese but there are many others to choose from. If you can't find Ribblesdale, trust your taste buds and go for something you like. If you enjoy it, the chances are other people will too.

Gregg Wallace, Masterchef Judge

1 Preheat the oven to 180°C/350°F/Gas Mark 4.

2 Remove the stalks from the figs. Cut a deep cross in the top of each fig and arrange them snugly in a small, buttered baking dish. Drizzle 2 tablespoons of the honey on top and bake for 8–10 minutes.

3 Meanwhile, cut a 10–12cm (4–5 in) circle from each piece of brioche and toast lightly on both sides. Mix the remaining honey and the peppercorns together.

4 Put the toast on a baking sheet and place the baked figs on top. Carefully tease open the top of each fig and place the cheese inside. Return to the oven for about 5 minutes, until the cheese has melted.

5 Transfer the figs and brioche to warm serving plates. Drizzle with the honey and pepper dressing and sprinkle the chives on top. Serve accompanied with the yoghurt.

'As far as being a professional is concerned, you need a passion for food … that is more important than anything else.'
Peter Richards, Masterchef Mentor

Pears with Roquefort, Rocket and Pickled Walnuts

This is a delicious combination of flavours, and there are several options for the presentation. For example, you could simply slice the pears and crumble the blue cheese over them, then make a dressing with the lemon and mascarpone. Be sure to include the pickled walnuts. They're a real treat.

→ 4 RIPE WILLIAM PEARS
→ JUICE OF 1 LEMON
→ 100G (4OZ) ROQUEFORT CHEESE
→ 100G (4OZ) MASCARPONE CHEESE
→ 200G (7OZ) WILD ROCKET
→ 3 TBSP EXTRA VIRGIN OLIVE OIL
→ A LITTLE GOOD-QUALITY AGED
   BALSAMIC VINEGAR
→ 16 PICKLED WALNUTS, DRAINED
→ SEA SALT AND FRESHLY GROUND
   BLACK PEPPER

1 Peel the pears, if liked, and remove the cores, leaving a fairly large cavity. Put the pears in a dish and squeeze the lemon juice over them.

2 Mix the Roquefort and mascarpone cheese together and season with plenty of freshly ground black pepper. Pipe the mixture into the pear cavities, or use a small teaspoon to stuff them.

3 Divide the rocket between 4 plates and sit a stuffed pear in the centre of each one.

4 Drizzle the oil and balsamic vinegar over the rocket and scatter the pickled walnuts around. Season with a little sea salt and black pepper and serve immediately.

Masterchef Masterclass
John Torode's Pasta

I know that it's easy to buy pasta and people generally can't be bothered with making it at home, but it is very satisfying to do. Once you know the basics, you can make all sorts of parcels and shapes. Although most of the dried pasta available in shops is of good quality, the vacuum-packed 'fresh' pasta is nothing like the stuff you can make yourself. Proper home-made fresh pasta is rich in eggs and has a lovely, supple texture.

It speeds up the process if you have a hand-cranked pasta machine for rolling out the dough (though with a bit of elbow grease, you can manage with a long rolling pin). A pasta machine is not expensive and it helps you to produce long, thin sheets of pasta in just a few minutes. It fixes to the worktop with a metal clamp and you then pass the dough between rollers until it reaches the thickness you require. There are also special cutters for producing ribbon shapes, such as pappardelle, fettuccine and tagliatelle.

Here are some guidelines for making successful pasta:

→ Use Italian '00' (doppio zero) flour, available in delicatessens and some supermarkets. It is high in gluten, whereas softer flours absorb too much liquid and the pasta may not be strong enough.
→ Pasta dough should be firm but not stiff and crumbly. If it is too soft, mix in a little more flour, a tablespoon at a time; if it is too stiff, mix in a little more egg or olive oil.
→ Cook pasta in a very large pan of boiling salted water, so it has plenty of room to move around and won't stick.
→ Fresh pasta cooks very quickly – sometimes in under a minute – so start checking it as soon as the water has returned to the boil.

John Torode's
Basic Pasta

MAKES ABOUT 600G (1LB 5OZ)

→ 500G (1LB 2OZ) ITALIAN '00' FLOUR, PLUS EXTRA FOR DUSTING
→ A PINCH OF TABLE SALT
→ 4 EGGS PLUS 3 EGG YOLKS, LIGHTLY BEATEN TOGETHER
→ 1 TBSP OLIVE OIL

1 Put the flour and salt into a food processor, add half the egg mixture and whiz until incorporated. Add the oil and whiz again.

2 Start to add the rest of the eggs a little at a time, stopping the machine regularly to feel the texture of the mixture. When it is ready, it will be like large, loose breadcrumbs that will come together into a dough if you squeeze them between your fingertips. You may not need to use all the egg, or you may even need to add a little more.

3 Tip the mixture out on to a floured work surface and push together into a ball. Knead for 1–2 minutes by pushing it away with the heel of your hand, folding it over and giving it a quarter turn. It should be smooth and elastic. Wrap in cling film and leave to rest for an hour.

4 Divide the dough into 6 pieces. Re-wrap 5 of them in cling film, then roll out the remaining one in a hand-cranked pasta machine. To do this, put the rollers of the machine on the widest setting. Flatten the piece of dough slightly, then run it through the machine 3 or 4 times, folding it in half each time and giving it a half turn before putting it through the machine again. The dough should become progressively smooth and silky. If it starts to stick, dust it lightly with flour. Repeat with the remaining pieces of dough.

5 Now feed each piece of dough through the machine without folding it, lowering the setting one notch at a time until you reach the required thickness (it's not usually necessary to go to the lowest setting).

6 Cut the rolled pasta into whatever shape you like; you can use the pasta machine attachment to cut them into ribbons.

John Torode's Pappardelle with Chicken Liver Sauce

SERVES 6

- → 600G (1LB 5OZ) FRESH PASTA (SEE OPPOSITE)
- → 3 TBSP OLIVE OIL
- → 500G (1LB 2OZ) CHICKEN LIVERS, TRIMMED
- → 2 ONIONS, SLICED
- → 2 SPRIGS OF OREGANO, CHOPPED
- → 1 RED CHILLI, FINELY CHOPPED
- → 3 GARLIC CLOVES, FINELY CHOPPED
- → 2 X 400G (14OZ) CANS OF TOMATOES, COARSELY CHOPPED
- → 1 GLASS OF RED WINE
- → A GOOD HANDFUL OF PARSLEY, CHOPPED
- → 15G (½OZ) BUTTER
- → SALT AND FRESHLY GROUND BLACK PEPPER
- → FRESHLY GRATED PARMESAN CHEESE, TO SERVE

Pasta and chicken livers may seem a little weird but it is actually a very old combination. You may have come across bruschetta or crostini topped with chopped chicken livers. This sauce is based on the same principle but then mixed with wonderful, thick-cut fresh pasta. You could also serve it with gnocchi.

1 Roll out the pasta as described opposite and cut it into pappardelle (strips about 2cm (³/₄ in) wide).

2 Heat 2 tablespoons of the olive oil in a large frying pan, add the chicken livers and fry over a fairly high heat for about 1 minute. Toss well and fry for 2 minutes longer, until well coloured and crisp on the outside but still pink on the inside. Remove from the pan and set aside.

3 Add the remaining olive oil to the pan and add the onions and oregano. Fry until the onions are translucent, then add the chilli and garlic and fry for another minute. Stir in the chopped tomatoes, red wine and some salt and pepper. Simmer for 5 minutes, stirring frequently, then increase the heat to high and cook for a minute or two longer, until the sauce thickens.

4 Cook the pasta in a large pan of boiling salted water until *al dente* (tender but firm to the bite), then drain. Set aside, with the warm pan.

5 Chop the livers roughly and add to the sauce with the parsley. Taste and adjust the seasoning.

6 Return the pasta to the warm pan and toss with the butter, then add the sauce and toss well. Serve with Parmesan cheese.

Inspired by contestant Jonny Batie

Thai-style Pork Cakes

Little Thai fish cakes have become de rigueur at finger-food parties and so they should be – tasty and easy to handle, they can be prepared well in advance. These little pork cakes fit the same criteria. The key to keeping them moist is to use fish sauce to season them instead of salt. The addition of water also helps keep the meat moist and stops it becoming grainy and sandy when cooked.

→ 2 SPRING ONIONS, FINELY CHOPPED

→ 2.5CM (1 IN) PIECE OF FRESH GINGER, FINELY CHOPPED

→ 1 LARGE, MILD RED CHILLI, FINELY CHOPPED

→ A GOOD HANDFUL OF CORIANDER LEAVES AND STALKS, FINELY CHOPPED

→ 400G (14OZ) MINCED PORK

→ 2 TSP THAI FISH SAUCE (*NAM PLA*)

→ 1 TSP SESAME OIL

→ 100ML (3½FL OZ) VEGETABLE OIL

→ 4 TBSP SWEET CHILLI SAUCE

→ 4 TBSP ROASTED SALTED PEANUTS, CHOPPED

→ 12 LARGE ICEBERG LETTUCE LEAVES

→ 2 LIMES, CUT INTO WEDGES

ⓜ MASTERCHEF TOP TIP

If possible, use a mortar and pestle to pound the herbs and aromatics. This will bruise them, releasing the juices and flavours that enhance the beauty of this Thai dish.
Peter Richards, Masterchef Mentor

1 Put the spring onions, ginger, chilli and coriander into a pestle and mortar or a food processor and pound to a paste, adding a little water if necessary.

2 Put the paste into a mixing bowl, add the pork, fish sauce and sesame oil and mix well. Add 50ml (2fl oz) of cold water and beat thoroughly to blend all the ingredients together. Chill for 10 minutes.

3 Shape the mixture into 12 patties, about 2cm (¾ in) thick and 5cm (2 in) in diameter.

4 Heat the vegetable oil in a heavy-based frying pan over a medium heat. Put the patties in the hot oil and fry gently for 3–4 minutes on each side, until well coloured and fragrant. Drain on kitchen paper.

5 Put the sweet chilli sauce in a small bowl and the chopped peanuts in another. Serve the patties on a large platter with the chilli sauce, peanuts, lettuce leaves and lime wedges. To eat, place a pork patty on a lettuce leaf and sprinkle with chopped peanuts. Add a little sweet chilli sauce and lime juice, then wrap the leaf around the patty.

Inspired by contestant Thomasina Miers

Chicken Mousse and Cobnut Ravioli

It doesn't occur to many people to make ravioli but it is a real joy to do – quite soothing, as it takes time and patience. This recipe is definitely worth the trouble.

Serves 6
- → 100G (4OZ) SKINLESS CHICKEN BREAST, CHOPPED
- → 2 MEDIUM EGG YOLKS
- → 150ML (¼ PINT) WHIPPING CREAM
- → ¼ TSP GROUND ALLSPICE
- → ¼ TSP GROUND MACE
- → 50G (2OZ) COBNUTS OR HAZELNUTS, TOASTED AND CHOPPED
- → 50G (2OZ) FOIE GRAS
- → SALT AND FRESHLY GROUND BLACK PEPPER

For the pasta:
- → 300G (11OZ) ITALIAN '00' FLOUR
- → 3 LARGE EGGS

To serve:
- → 50G (2OZ) CLARIFIED BUTTER
- → 4 SAGE LEAVES
- → A SMALL KNOB OF SALTED BUTTER
- → 25G (1OZ) PARMESAN CHEESE, FRESHLY GRATED

1 To make the pasta, put the flour and eggs into a food processor and process until they come together into a large ball. Remove and knead by hand on a lightly floured surface for 1–2 minutes until smooth and elastic. Wrap in cling film and chill for 1 hour.

2 While the dough is resting, make the filling. Put the chicken and egg yolks in the food processor and process to a paste. Transfer to a mixing bowl and chill for 10 minutes. Remove from the fridge and whisk in the cream and spices. Season well with salt and some black pepper. Add the cobnuts and stir well to combine. Return the mixture to the fridge while you roll out the pasta.

3 Divide the dough into 3 pieces. Re-wrap 2 pieces and place the third on a floured work surface. Flatten it out by hand into a rectangle, then roll it out to about 20cm (8 in) wide and 45cm (18 in) long using a rolling pin or a pasta machine (see page 30). Cut the pasta sheet lengthways in half to give 2 strips 10cm (4 in) wide.

4 Place heaped teaspoons of the chicken mousse at 5cm (2 in) intervals along the centre of one sheet of pasta and then push a tiny ball of foie gras into the centre of the mousse. Brush a little water along the edges of the sheet and between the heaps of filling. Lay the second sheet of pasta on top and press it down firmly around the filling and along the edges. Cut out the ravioli using a sharp knife or a ravioli wheel. Repeat with the remaining dough and filling, laying the ravioli on lightly floured baking sheets.

5 To cook the ravioli, bring a large pan of salted water to the boil. Reduce the heat to a gentle boil, add the ravioli and bring back to a simmer. Cook for 3–4 minutes, then remove with a slotted spoon.

6 Meanwhile, heat the clarified butter in a small pan over a high heat. Deep-fry the sage leaves for 30 seconds, then remove and place on kitchen paper to drain. Add the salted butter to the pan.

7 Divide the ravioli between 4 dishes and drizzle with the butter. Garnish with the Parmesan and sage leaves and serve at once.

Inspired by contestant Caroline Brewester

Chicken Liver Parfait with Caramelised Onions

This parfait is much simpler than usual. For most parfaits, the raw mixture is puréed and then baked in a bain marie, but here Caroline has simply fried the chicken livers first and then puréed them. Leftovers will keep in the fridge for about 3 days.

Serves 10
→ 100G (4OZ) CLARIFIED BUTTER
→ 50G (2OZ) SHALLOTS, DICED
→ 450G (1LB) FRESH CHICKEN
   LIVERS, TRIMMED
→ 2 TBSP BRANDY
→ 2 TBSP DOUBLE CREAM
→ 300G (11OZ) BUTTER
→ A HANDFUL OF LAMB'S LETTUCE
→ SALT AND FRESHLY
   GROUND BLACK PEPPER
→ TOAST, TO SERVE
For the caramelised onions:
→ 300G (11OZ) ONIONS, FINELY SLICED
→ 1 TBSP OLIVE OIL
→ 1 TSP SUGAR
→ 2 TSP GOOD-QUALITY SHERRY VINEGAR

ⓜ MASTERCHEF TOP TIP
To slice the parfait, fill a tall jug with boiling water and leave a long, thin knife in it for a few minutes. Take the knife from the water and wipe it clean; the hot blade will now slide easily through the soft, buttery parfait.
John Torode, Masterchef Judge

1 Heat about a quarter of the clarified butter in a frying pan, add the shallots and fry over a medium heat until slightly browned. Transfer to a food processor.

2 Turn up the heat under the frying pan and add the rest of the clarified butter. Add the chicken livers and fry quickly so that they are browned on the outside but still pink in the middle. Transfer to the food processor.

3 Deglaze the pan by adding the brandy and stirring to scrape up any bits from the base of the pan. Raise the heat and simmer for a minute to boil off the alcohol, then add to the liver mixture, along with the double cream and some salt and pepper. Blitz to a rough paste.

4 Cut the butter into large lumps and add it to the mixture a lump at a time, with the food processor running on high. Then taste the mixture and adjust the seasoning if necessary (remember the flavour will be less strong when cold).

5 Sieve the mixture into a bowl, then transfer to a 450g (1lb) loaf tin lined with cling film. Chill for 12 hours to set.

6 For the caramelised onions, put the onions in a frying pan with 100ml (3½fl oz) water, the olive oil and a pinch of salt. Place over a very low heat and sweat for 30 minutes or until translucent and sweet but not coloured.

7 Add the sugar and cook over a medium heat until golden brown and caramelised. Add the sherry vinegar and simmer to reduce it slightly. Taste and adjust the amount of sugar or vinegar if necessary; it should have a good balance of sweet and sour.

8 Turn out the parfait and cut into thin slices. Garnish with lamb's lettuce and serve with the warm onions and some toast.

Inspired by contestant Mark Todd

Heston-inspired Foie Gras

Foie gras is usually cooked in a terrine or fried but, as Mark learned from Heston Blumenthal, chef-proprietor of The Fat Duck in Bray, it can also be cooked slowly in a bain marie, then coloured with a blowtorch. The result is delicious and meltingly tender.

- → 250G (9OZ) PIECE OF FOIE GRAS, VACUUM-PACKED
- → 10 ALMONDS, CHOPPED
- → 2 TBSP FINELY CHOPPED FLAT-LEAF PARSLEY
- → 2 TBSP FINELY SNIPPED CHIVES
- → A GOOD PINCH OF TABLE SALT
- → A GOOD PINCH OF ROCK SALT
- → ¼ TSP FRESHLY GROUND BLACK PEPPER
- → A GOOD-QUALITY CRUSTY FRENCH LOAF, TO SERVE

  For the kirsch sauce:
- → 25 RED CHERRIES
- → 1 TBSP CASTER SUGAR
- → 100ML (3½FL OZ) KIRSCH

 MASTERCHEF TOP TIP
Foie gras is the enlarged liver of a goose or duck. This enlargement is achieved by force-feeding the bird. In Roman times the birds were fed figs, but nowadays it is more likely to be corn. Duck foie gras is the favourite of most connoisseurs; it breaks down much better during cooking than that of a goose. When buying, always go for rounded, smooth liver. It should be as putty coloured as possible. Very yellow livers tend to be a bit grainy. Go on, dig in! A bit of luxury will do you good.
Gregg Wallace, Masterchef Judge

1 First make the sauce. Put the cherries, sugar and kirsch in a small, heavy-based saucepan. Bring to the boil, then reduce the heat and simmer for about 20 minutes, until the cherries are soft. Press the mixture through a fine sieve. Pour into a small serving dish and set aside.

2 Put the bag of foie gras into a large bowl of very hot, but not boiling, water and leave for 10 minutes. Drain off the water, which will be cooling down, and cover with more very hot water. Leave for 20 minutes.

3 Mix the almonds and herbs together and set aside.

4 Remove the foie gras from the packaging, discarding the liquid in the bag. Brown the foie gras with a blowtorch, then season with the table salt, rock salt and black pepper.

5 Press the almond and herb mixture over the top of the foie gras to make a crust. Slice the foie gras and divide between 4 serving plates. Serve with the cherry sauce drizzled around the plate and accompanied by the bread.

‘**I am going to win it ... I'm going to do my damnedest to win it, without a doubt.**’
Mark Todd, Contestant

Name: Anna Mosesson
Age: 48
Occupation: I am a Borough Market stall holder (I have been for 6 years); I sell Scandinavian food.
Place of residence: Suffolk
Why did you apply to Masterchef?
My son was at the market with me, and he saw these bits of paper being handed out and said, 'Mamma I think you should go for this!', so I did. A lot of people I know said, 'This is it, it's your open door.' I just thought that being a celebrity chef sounded better than working on a stall in Borough Market!
What do you cook at home and who do you cook for?
I cook for my family, for parties (my husband enjoys a good party, we love entertaining). I cook a lot of Scandinavian dishes and I like to experiment.
What is your favourite meal?
My favourite meal is fettuccini with white truffle and a little butter and black pepper, I just love it! And I love Muscat grapes if I want something sweet.
What are your aspirations in the world of cooking and food?
I was disappointed not to get through to the next round of Masterchef. I would love to be a TV presenter. In the meantime, I'm going to open a restaurant in Borough Market and take on a Swedish chef – I'm going to decorate it and contribute a lot of my ideas. It's my baby, it's going to happen.

Name: Daksha Mistry
Age: 45
Occupation: Trying to be a chef! At the moment, I cook for friends and family.
Place of residence: London
Why did you apply to Masterchef?
It was a really good opportunity and I thought, 'If I don't try, I don't know where I'll be.' My husband really encouraged me: he said it was an opportunity knocking, so I applied on the Internet. I went on Masterchef to show people that Indian food is not about the chicken tikka masala, korma and vindaloo that you get in Indian restaurants in the UK – these dishes don't even exist in India.
What do you cook at home and who do you cook for?
I cook for friends and family, sometimes up to 100 people! I cook whatever they want – all Indian food, of course.
What is your favourite meal?
My favourite is actually my own version of Italian food! It's a fusion of Italian and Indian: I make a pasta dish with puréed aubergine with basil, coriander, cumin, garlic and ginger poured over the pasta – that's my favourite.
What are your aspirations in the world of cooking and food?
My aim is to do a cookery show on television, to show people how to cook in the style of my region of India (Gujarat). I specialize in this cooking and I speak Gujarati. I'm convinced that one day I will do this.

Name: Katherine Haworth
Age: 47
Occupation: Freelance housekeeper and amateur cook.
Place of residence: Nineteen miles north of York
Why did you apply to Masterchef?
Because I really wanted to do something with my cooking, take it further and show the world I could cook, and then hopefully get some work as a cook.
What do you cook at home and who do you cook for?
I cook for my husband, my friends and my relatives. I cook absolutely everything. I particularly love Italian and Moroccan flavours. The only thing I never, ever cook is tripe (I even occasionally cook liver for the dog!).
What is your favourite meal?
I've got so many – it depends on the time of year. My absolute favourite is the simplest thing you could possibly think of: half a dozen oysters, some top-quality smoked salmon with some caviar, followed by a crème brûlée and accompanied by a bottle of the best bubbly. That's what we have for a real celebration.
What are your aspirations in the world of cooking and food?
I'd really love to be a recipe developer, or run a small, high-quality guest house.

Inspired by contestant Thomasina Miers

Flash-baked Mackerel with Beetroot Tzatsiki

Mackerel is a very underrated fish. It's delicious simply baked in the way that Thomasina has cooked it here. As mackerel is oily, it can also benefit from being cooked on a ridged griddle pan over a very high heat to char it slightly. This would work well with the sweet and sour tzatsiki.

→ 2 RAW BEETROOT
→ 1 TBSP GRATED FRESH HORSERADISH (OR USE GRATED HORSERADISH FROM A JAR)
→ 1 GARLIC CLOVE, CRUSHED
→ 1 TBSP CHOPPED DILL
→ 1 TBSP CHOPPED MINT
→ 150G (5OZ) GREEK-STYLE YOGHURT
→ 2 TSP CUMIN SEEDS, DRY-ROASTED AND GROUND
→ JUICE OF 1 LEMON
→ 2 X 350G (12OZ) MACKEREL, FILLETED
→ 2 TBSP CHOPPED PARSLEY
→ FRESHLY GROUND BLACK PEPPER

1 Preheat the oven to 220°C/425°F/Gas Mark 7.

2 Cook the beetroot in boiling salted water until tender, then drain. When cool enough to handle, peel the beetroot and grate it into a bowl.

3 Add the horseradish, garlic, herbs, yoghurt, half the ground cumin, half the lemon juice and some black pepper. Mix well, then set aside.

4 Put the mackerel fillets on a baking tray lined with lightly oiled greaseproof paper and season with black pepper. Bake for 4–5 minutes, until the flesh turns opaque and flakes easily.

5 Transfer the fillets to warm serving plates and sprinkle over the parsley and the remaining cumin and lemon juice. Serve immediately with the beetroot tzatsiki.

'Cumin, lemon and parsley always work so beautifully together ... this is delicious.'
John Torode, Masterchef Judge

Inspired by contestant Jacqueline Hillier

Lime Fried Squid with Mild Harissa

There are only two methods of cooking squid – very quickly or braised slowly over a long period. Anything in between and the squid will be tough. Try to avoid washing the squid in water when preparing it, as this takes away the wonderful sea flavour that is so endearing about squid. Instead, use a knife to scrap away any slime or sand. Although you won't need all the harissa in this recipe, it keeps well in the fridge.

- 200G (7OZ) PREPARED SQUID, WITH TENTACLES
- 2 TBSP GROUNDNUT OIL
- 200G (7OZ) ROCKET
- A SMALL BUNCH OF CORIANDER, ROUGHLY CHOPPED
- SALT AND FRESHLY GROUND BLACK PEPPER

For the harissa:
- 5 MILD LONG RED CHILLIES
- 2 GARLIC CLOVES, PEELED
- 1 LARGE RED PEPPER, HALVED AND DESEEDED
- 2 TSP CARAWAY SEEDS
- 2 TSP CUMIN SEEDS
- 2 TSP TOMATO PURÉE
- 1 TSP SMOKED PAPRIKA
- 2 TSP RED WINE VINEGAR
- 3 TBSP OLIVE OIL

For the lime dressing:
- 1 MILD LONG RED CHILLI, FINELY CHOPPED
- 2 GARLIC CLOVES, CRUSHED
- 1 TBSP SUGAR
- 1 TBSP THAI FISH SAUCE (NAM PLA)
- JUICE OF 1 LIME

1 For the harissa, purée all the ingredients except the vinegar and oil in a food processor. Transfer to a mixing bowl and stir in the vinegar and oil, then set aside.

2 For the dressing, pound the chilli, garlic and sugar to a paste in a pestle and mortar. Stir in the fish sauce and lime juice, then set aside.

3 Cut the squid into 1cm (½ in) rings and divide up the clusters of tentacles. Toss in half the groundnut oil and season well with salt and pepper.

4 Heat a large, heavy-based frying pan until it is very hot. Pour the remaining oil into the pan and add the squid, spreading it out in a single layer. Sear the squid for 30 seconds, without shaking the pan. Toss the pan once and sear for another 30 seconds over the highest possible heat. Repeat twice, then remove the squid from the pan. As long as the pan remains very hot, the squid will be cooked through and tender.

5 Put the rocket and coriander in a large bowl. Add half the lime dressing and arrange on a serving plate. Drizzle a little of the harissa around the plate. Pile the squid on the salad leaves and sprinkle with the remaining lime dressing. Serve while the squid is still warm.

Inspired by contestant Scott Ball

Seared Scallops with Wild Mushroom Sauté

Two expensive ingredients in one dish, but this is a real treat and a perfect autumn or Christmas starter. Scott came up with some great combinations – the sign of a clever cook who understands the fundamental rules of cookery. Many people try that little bit too hard, whereas this recipe does not. The flavours are perfectly balanced, with the salty scallops and rich mushrooms all held together by the sharpness of crème fraîche and the fresh thyme.

→ 50G (2OZ) BUTTER
→ 2 SHALLOTS, FINELY DICED
→ 1 GARLIC CLOVE, CRUSHED
→ 300G (11OZ) MIXED WILD MUSHROOMS, CUT IN HALF IF LARGE
→ LEAVES FROM A SPRIG OF THYME
→ 100ML (3½FL OZ) CHAMPAGNE OR DRY WHITE WINE
→ 5 TBSP CRÈME FRAÎCHE
→ A LITTLE VEGETABLE OIL FOR BRUSHING
→ 12 LARGE SCALLOPS
→ 3–4 TBSP CHOPPED FLAT-LEAF PARSLEY
→ SALT AND FRESHLY GROUND BLACK PEPPER

1 Melt the butter in a heavy-based frying pan, add the shallots and cook until soft and translucent. Stir in the garlic and mushrooms and cook for 3 minutes over a medium heat.

2 Add the thyme leaves and the champagne or white wine. Cook for 2 minutes, until slightly reduced, then remove the mushrooms with a slotted spoon and keep warm. Stir the crème fraîche into the cooking liquor and bring to the boil. Simmer until reduced and slightly thickened, then return the mushrooms to the pan and season to taste.

3 Lightly brush a heavy-based frying pan with a little vegetable oil and place it over a high heat until very hot. Season the scallops with a little salt, place them in the hot pan and sear for 1 minute on each side, until browned and lightly caramelised.

4 Pour the mushroom sauce over the scallops. Stir in the parsley, heat through and serve.

'It's not often that I've had soy sauce, potato, apple and feta cheese on the same plate!'
John Torode, Masterchef Judge, to a contestant

Scallops on a Minted Pea Purée

A classic combination, and one that is served at Kensington Place restaurant in London when peas come into season. The pea purée is surprisingly sweet and needs to be knocked down a touch by some lemon – either serve with lemon wedges or use lemon juice to season the purée.

→ 300ML (½ PINT) GOOD-QUALITY CHICKEN STOCK
→ A SMALL BUNCH OF MINT LEAVES, STALKS REMOVED
→ 3 TBSP OLIVE OIL
→ 1 ONION, FINELY CHOPPED
→ 500G (1LB 2OZ) FROZEN PEAS
→ A PINCH OF SUGAR
→ A LITTLE VEGETABLE OIL FOR BRUSHING
→ 12 KING SCALLOPS
→ SALT AND FRESHLY GROUND BLACK PEPPER
→ LEMON WEDGES, TO GARNISH

1 Bring the chicken stock to the boil in a small saucepan. Finely chop about a third of the mint leaves and set aside.

2 Heat the olive oil in a large frying pan, add the onion and cook gently until soft and translucent. Stir in the whole mint leaves and cook briefly until wilted.

3 Add the chicken stock and bring back to the boil. Stir in the frozen peas, bring to the boil, then reduce the heat and simmer for 3 minutes until the peas are just cooked. Strain the pea and onion mixture, reserving the liquid.

4 Purée the peas in a food processor, adding a little of the reserved stock. The purée should be quite thick. Spoon the purée into a saucepan and warm through gently. Season with the sugar and some salt and pepper, then sprinkle in the finely chopped mint. Keep warm.

5 Lightly brush a ridged griddle pan or a heavy-based frying pan with a little vegetable oil and place it over a high heat until very hot. Season the scallops with a little salt, place them in the hot pan and sear for 1 minute on each side, until browned and lightly caramelised.

6 Divide the pea purée between 4 plates and place the scallops on top. Serve immediately, garnished with lemon wedges.

'I love food like this, because it's really honest. It has great ingredients and has been cooked very simply.'
John Torode, Masterchef Judge

Inspired by contestant Daksha Mistry

Prawn Puris

A puri is a deep-fried unleavened bread from India. Here the prawn filling takes the dish from standard spiced fare to a great combination of tastes, textures and aromas. If you decide not to cook the whole recipe, make the puris and eat them plain.

→ 2 GARLIC CLOVES, ROUGHLY CHOPPED
→ 2.5CM (1 IN) PIECE OF FRESH GINGER, ROUGHLY CHOPPED
→ 2 GREEN CHILLIES, ROUGHLY CHOPPED
→ 2 LEMONGRASS STALKS
→ 1 LITRE (1¾ PINTS) VEGETABLE OIL FOR DEEP-FRYING
→ 8 RAW KING PRAWNS
→ A KNOB OF GHEE OR CLARIFIED BUTTER
→ ½ TSP GROUND BLACK PEPPER
→ ½ TSP GROUND CUMIN
→ ½ TSP GROUND CORIANDER
→ 2 SPRING ONIONS, CUT ON THE DIAGONAL INTO SLICES 5MM (¼ IN) THICK
→ 1 TSP TOMATO PURÉE
→ 2-3 TBSP CHOPPED FRESH CORIANDER
→ 2 TBSP CHOPPED MINT
→ 2 LIMES
→ A FEW SALAD LEAVES, TO GARNISH
For the dough:
→ 225G (8OZ) SELF-RAISING FLOUR
→ A PINCH OF SALT
→ 25G (1OZ) GHEE OR CLARIFIED BUTTER

Ⓜ **MASTERCHEF TOP TIP**
Puris can be made in advance and frozen, which is useful if you are preparing an Indian meal. The balance of herbs and spices is most important in this dish. Make sure they are all absolutely fresh and unblemished, as this will affect the end result.
Peter Richards, Masterchef Mentor

1 To make the dough, sift the flour and salt into a bowl, and rub in the ghee or butter with your fingertips. Make a well in the centre and gradually add about 150ml (¼ pint) water until you have a stiff dough. Cover with a damp cloth and leave for 20 minutes.

2 Put the garlic, ginger and chillies in a pestle and mortar or a food processor and grind to a smooth paste. Set aside.

3 Peel away the dry outer layers of the lemongrass until you reach the tender core. Crush and chop finely, then set aside.

4 After 20 minutes, knead the dough for 1–2 minutes, until smooth. Divide it into 8 and shape each piece into a ball. On a floured board, roll out each ball into a circle about 10cm (4 in) in diameter.

5 Heat the vegetable oil in a wok or deep-fat fryer until nearly smoking. Fry the puris, one or two at a time, until golden on both sides. Stack the puris in a colander lined with kitchen paper, then cover and keep warm.

6 Shell the prawns, then cut along the back, slicing about halfway through the flesh. With the tip of the knife, remove the dark intestinal vein along the back, then open the prawns out.

7 Put the ghee or clarified butter, black pepper, cumin and ground coriander in a frying pan and gently fry the spices for 1 minute. Stir in the garlic, chilli and ginger paste and cook for 2 minutes. Add the prawns and cook for 2 minutes. Stir in the spring onions, tomato purée, lemongrass and chopped herbs and fry for 4 minutes, until the prawns are cooked. Add the juice of 1 lime, stir well and remove from the heat.

8 Pile the salad leaves on to 4 plates. Divide the prawn mixture between the puris. Loosely fold each puri in half and place on the leaves. Cut up the remaining lime and use as garnish. Serve at once.

Fish and Shellfish

Fillet of Sea Trout on Asian Leaves

Wonderfully fresh salads such as this one are the base of a great many Asian dishes. It's a good one to keep in mind to use not only with fish but also with shellfish, such as prawns or roast lobster.

→ A LARGE BUNCH OF CORIANDER
→ A SMALL BUNCH OF MINT
→ 16 CHERRY TOMATOES, QUARTERED
→ 2 SHALLOTS, THINLY SLICED
→ 2 TSP PLAIN FLOUR
→ 4 X 150G (5OZ) THICK FILLETS OF SEA TROUT, SKIN ON (USE TAIL END OF SALMON IF SEA TROUT IS NOT AVAILABLE)
→ 2 TBSP VEGETABLE OIL
→ SEA SALT

For the dressing:
→ 1 LONG RED CHILLI, DESEEDED AND CHOPPED
→ 2 TSP CASTER SUGAR
→ 1 TBSP LIME JUICE
→ 2 TSP SESAME OIL
→ 2 TSP THAI FISH SAUCE (*NAM PLA*)

MASTERCHEF TOP TIP

When cooking an oily pink fish such as trout or salmon, dry the skin well before placing it in the hot pan. Do not shake the pan during cooking or the flesh will tear from the skin. Leave the fish to cook over a high heat for a good 3 minutes, until the edges of the skin begin to brown and the fish can be easily lifted away from the hot surface.

John Torode, Masterchef Judge

1 First prepare the dressing. Pound the red chilli and sugar to a paste in a pestle and mortar. Add the lime juice, sesame oil and fish sauce and mix together well. The dressing should taste sweet, sour, salty and hot. Adjust the balance of ingredients, if necessary.

2 Roughly tear the coriander and mint leaves and mix them with the tomatoes and shallots. Chill until ready to serve.

3 Season the flour with a little sea salt and lightly dust the trout fillets in it.

4 Place a large, heavy-based frying pan over a high heat. When the pan is hot, add the vegetable oil. Place the fish fillets in the pan skin-side down and cook for about 3 minutes, until golden and crisp. Turn the fish over and cook for a further 2–3 minutes, until the flesh is opaque and firm to the touch. Remove from the heat.

5 Toss a little of the dressing with the salad. Arrange the salad on 4 plates and place the trout fillets on top. Drizzle with a little more dressing and serve immediately.

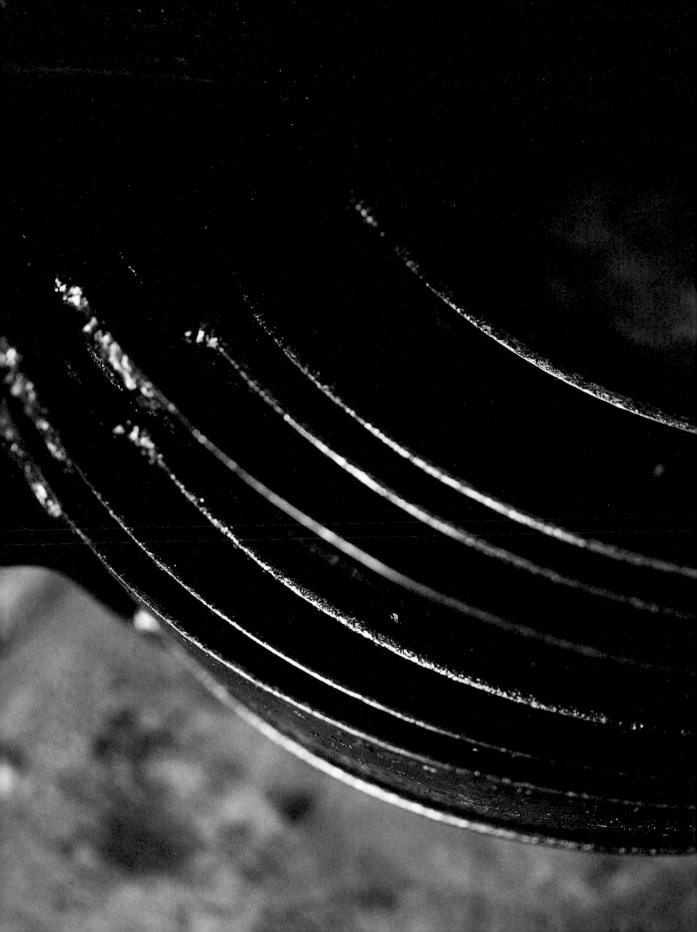

Masterchef Masterclass
John Torode's Flat Fish

First, a few fish facts. Like most produce, fish are seasonal. In general, they are best in the winter months, after they have had time to recover from the spawning season. They fall into two main categories – flat and round – and are further categorised by the type of water they come from: deep, shallow, cold or warm.

Flat fish live on the bottom of the ocean and bury themselves in the sand, camouflaged against predators, awaiting their prey. They are mostly thin, so the smaller ones should, if possible, be cooked on the bone, which will conduct the heat from the inside, helping the delicate flesh to cook more quickly and stay moist.

Round fish, such as cod, salmon, sea bass, haddock and hake, are very active, searching the seas for food and swimming huge distances to mate and spawn. Because of this they grow at a faster rate than flat fish and have large hunks of delicious, dense flesh, fantastic for fillets or steaks.

Many of the best-known flat fish – sole, plaice, turbot, skate and brill – are indigenous to UK waters, yet as a rule people aren't very confident about choosing and preparing them. Here are some points to consider when buying fish.

→ Avoid pre-packaged fish, as there is usually a piece of absorbent paper in the bottom of the tray, which can suck the moisture from the flesh, leaving it dry and pappy.

→ Find a good local fishmonger, or get to know the staff on your supermarket fish counter and check that the fish hasn't been fresh-frozen, then defrosted. When a fish is frozen, the water cells expand, then when it is defrosted they collapse, forcing out the water, so that the cooked texture can be dry and chalky.

→ The best fish counters have whole fish on display, so you can check that the eyes are clear and shiny and the gills moist – it's much more difficult to judge the age and condition of fish that has already been cut into fillets or steaks. The skin should shimmer, but beware of any fish whose flesh has a rainbow hue. This shows that it is old – not off, but past its prime.

→ Look for line-caught fish where you can, as this is a way of protesting against the massive dredgers that rape the seas of all that lies in their way.

John Torode's
Filleting flat fish

A good fishmonger will fillet fish for you but it's still worth knowing how to do this at home. The following technique applies to all flat fish.

1 Lay the fish on a chopping board, dark skin up, with the head at the front of the board. Using your finger, feel down the centre of the fish to trace the backbone. Once you are comfortable with the anatomy, use a sharp knife to cut around the collar of the fish on the ungutted side.

2 Trace the backbone down the centre of the fish with the knife, keeping to the same side as the top incision and pressing gently down on the bone so the knife starts to prise the flesh from the bone.

3 Re-angle the knife to about 90 degrees and, starting from the head, carefully run the knife from top to bottom, releasing the flesh from the bones. Do this 3 or 4 times until the fillet comes free.

4 Repeat the process with the other side, then turn the fish over and start again.

5 To remove the skin, place the fillet on the board, skin side down, with the thin end towards you. Grasp the thin end in your left hand, if right handed (vice versa if not).

6 Pass the knife through the flesh at this point until the resistance of the skin stops the knife. Then tilt the knife flat so it is almost parallel to the skin and no flesh is sitting between blade and skin. With a slow, see-sawing motion, pull the skin with your left hand and push with the right, so the flesh is cut from the skin. As you work along the fillet, you can flip the flesh over to make it easier to see where you are cutting.

John Torode's
Cooking flat fish

The best way to cook fillets of flat fish is to shallow-fry them quickly in lots of butter, then serve them simply, with a wedge of lemon and perhaps some mashed potato (see pages 58–9) and wilted spinach. They shouldn't take more than three minutes to cook, but it's vital that you follow a few golden rules:

→ Because fish is so delicate, it should be fried with the skin on. This will protect the flesh and release essential oils that will improve the flavour and texture. You can always remove the skin once the fish has been cooked, if you prefer.

→ Fish should always be cooked over a high heat to seal the outside, keeping the juices locked inside. Season with salt and pepper before cooking but, once seasoned, don't leave it for too long before applying heat, as the salt will draw out the moisture from the flesh.

→ And remember, the most important rule of all is, don't overcook! Fish is made up of proteins that change and 'cook' when subjected to heat, salt or acid. In the case of heat, the fish will hold on to that heat, continuing to cook even after it has been taken from the pan, so you may have to experiment a little with the cooking times, taking the fish from the heat a minute or two before you think it is ready.

1 Melt 50g (2oz) butter in a large, heavy-based pan over a fairly high heat.

2 Season the fish well and place it in the pan, flesh side down; this is known as the presentation side, as it is the side that will be showing when the fish is served.

3 Cook for about 2 minutes, until the flesh is translucent but not coloured, then turn quickly but gently and cook for another minute, until the skin is lightly browned. When the fish is ready it will be just firm to the touch. Serve straight away, with a wedge of lemon.

Zarzuela

If you love food that is gutsy and full of punchy flavours, yet comforting and moreish at the same time, then this is the stew for you. What a dish! Chunks of tender white fish mixed with prawns, clams and mussels, are cooked with tomatoes and chilli. Serve with crusty bread, some garlic mayonnaise (see page 118) and extra chilli to push this dish to the very limits of culinary excellence.

→ 7 TBSP OLIVE OIL
→ 1 LARGE SPANISH ONION, FINELY CHOPPED
→ 2 LARGE, RIPE TOMATOES, SKINNED, DESEEDED AND FINELY CHOPPED
→ ½ TSP PIMENTON OR PAPRIKA
→ 2 THIN SLICES OF BREAD, CRUSTS REMOVED
→ 4 ALMONDS, TOASTED AND SKINNED
→ 3 GARLIC CLOVES, PEELED
→ 100G (4OZ) THICK COD FILLET, SKINNED
→ 100G (4OZ) MONKFISH FILLET, SKINNED
→ 100G (4OZ) HALIBUT FILLET, SKINNED
→ 1½ TBSP PLAIN FLOUR
→ 100G PREPARED SQUID, SLICED
→ 8 RAW TIGER PRAWNS
→ 16 MUSSELS, SCRUBBED AND DE-BEARDED
→ 8 LARGE CLAMS, SCRUBBED
→ 100ML (3½FL OZ) SPANISH BRANDY OR OTHER INEXPENSIVE BRANDY
→ 150ML (¼ PINT) DRY WHITE WINE
→ 2 TBSP CHOPPED PARSLEY
→ SALT AND FRESHLY GROUND BLACK PEPPER
→ CRUSTY BREAD, TO SERVE

Ⓜ MASTERCHEF TOP TIP

White mussels are nearly always boys, and yellow/orange ones girls. The season for European mussels is autumn and winter. Before you buy mussels, pick them up and tap them – they should feel full. Hollow-sounding shells mean scrawny molluscs. I like fishmongers who open up a few so you can see how meaty they are. Never buy a cracked one, and when you are cleaning them discard any open ones that don't close completely when you tap them.

Gregg Wallace, Masterchef Judge

1 Heat 3 tablespoons of the oil in a frying pan, add the onion and fry slowly until light golden. Add the tomatoes and pimenton and cook over a low heat until the oil separates from the vegetables and appears on the surface. Put to one side.

2 Heat 1 tablespoon of the oil in a separate frying pan, add the bread and fry on both sides until golden. Place in a mortar with the almonds, 2 cloves of garlic and 1 tablespoon of olive oil. Pound together to a fine paste, then set aside.

3 Season the cod, monkfish and halibut and dust them with the flour, shaking off any excess. Heat the remaining olive oil in a large frying pan and brown the fish in it separately – first the cod, then the monkfish, halibut, squid and prawns. As each is cooked, transfer to a large casserole.

4 Add the mussels and clams to the casserole. Chop the remaining clove of garlic and stir it into the casserole dish. Put over a low heat, pour the brandy over the fish and heat gently, then set it alight, standing well back.

5 When the flames have died down, stir in the reserved tomato mixture, followed by the white wine and just enough hot water to cover. Bring to the boil, then reduce the heat, cover and simmer for about 4 minutes, until the mussels and clams have opened. Discard any that remain closed.

6 Mix in the reserved bread paste to thicken the sauce, then add the parsley. Season to taste. Serve in large bowls, accompanied by crusty bread.

Seared Salmon with Lemon Beurre Blanc and Spinach

This is a real classic: salmon and a rich, buttery sauce with a little spinach. Unlike hollandaise sauce, which can be a bit heavy with fish because the egg yolks make it so rich, beurre blanc is soft and velvety but punchy at the same time.

→ A GOOD KNOB OF BUTTER
→ 2 SHALLOTS, FINELY DICED
→ ¼ TSP GRATED NUTMEG
→ 250G (9OZ) BABY SPINACH
→ 4 X 150G (5OZ) SALMON STEAKS
→ 2 TBSP OLIVE OIL
→ 4 TBSP DRY WHITE WINE
→ 1 LEMON, CUT INTO WEDGES
→ SALT AND FRESHLY GROUND BLACK PEPPER

For the lemon beurre blanc:
→ 1 SHALLOT, FINELY CHOPPED
→ 2 TBSP WHITE WINE VINEGAR
→ 2 TBSP LEMON JUICE
→ 4 TBSP DRY WHITE WINE
→ 85ML (3FL OZ) FISH STOCK OR WATER
→ 2 TBSP DOUBLE CREAM
→ 175G (6OZ) UNSALTED BUTTER, DICED
→ SALT AND WHITE PEPPER

MASTERCHEF TOP TIP
For best results when you make the sauce, the butter should be at room temperature and cut into 2cm (¾ in) chunks. Once the sauce is ready, it should ideally be used straight away, but if you leave it somewhere warm and stir it occasionally it should keep for a little while without separating.
John Torode, Masterchef Judge

1 Preheat the oven to 200°C/400°F/Gas Mark 6.

2 For the beurre blanc, put the shallot, vinegar, lemon juice, wine and fish stock or water into a small saucepan and bring to the boil. Reduce the heat and simmer until most of the liquid has evaporated. Add the cream and simmer over a high heat until reduced by half.

3 Lower the heat and gradually whisk in the butter a little at a time, to give a smooth sauce. Season with salt and white pepper, remove from the heat and keep warm.

4 Melt the knob of butter in a saucepan, add the shallots and cook gently until soft and translucent. Stir in the nutmeg and then add the spinach. Cook until wilted, then remove from the heat, cover and keep warm.

5 Season the salmon steaks. Heat the oil in an ovenproof frying pan over a high heat, add the salmon and sear on both sides for 1–2 minutes, until lightly browned.

6 Remove from the heat and pour in the wine. Transfer the pan to the oven and cook for about 5 minutes, until the fish is done.

7 Divide the spinach between 4 warmed plates and place a salmon steak on top of each one. Drizzle the lemon beurre blanc sauce on and around the salmon. Serve immediately, with the lemon wedges.

Red Mullet with Purple Broccoli and Courgette Gratin

This bright and vibrant dish has bags of flavour. Red mullet is a wonderfully oily, intensely flavoured fish that is eaten in huge amounts on the coast of France and Spain. It should always be very fresh, so be sure to buy yours from a good fishmonger.

- 16–20 CHARLOTTE POTATOES, PEELED
- 100G (4OZ) CLARIFIED BUTTER
- 85ML (3FL OZ) WHITE WINE
- 1 TBSP WHITE WINE VINEGAR
- 2 TBSP GREEN CHARTREUSE
- 75G (3OZ) BUTTER
- 4 MEDIUM RED MULLET, FILLETED
- A LITTLE SALMON ROE, TO GARNISH (OPTIONAL)
- 4 SPRIGS OF CHERVIL
- SALT AND FRESHLY GROUND BLACK PEPPER

For the gratin:
- 400G (14OZ) LARGE COURGETTES
- 400G (14OZ) PURPLE SPROUTING BROCCOLI
- 15G (½OZ) BUTTER
- A GOOD PINCH OF PAPRIKA
- 2 TBSP DOUBLE CREAM
- A GOOD PINCH OF GRATED NUTMEG

MASTERCHEF TOP TIP

To make clarified butter, simply put the butter in a heavy-based pan and heat gently until melted. Raise the heat and bring to the boil, then remove from the heat and leave for 10 minutes. The solids will fall to the bottom and the clarified butter (the liquid yellow fat) can be taken from the top.

John Torode, Masterchef Judge

1 Cook the potatoes in boiling salted water until semi-tender, then drain. Melt the clarified butter in a large frying pan, add the potatoes and cook for 8–10 minutes, until evenly browned, crisp on the outside and soft inside. Season to taste and keep warm.

2 For the gratin, finely slice half the courgettes, preferably using a mandoline. Blanch them for 30 seconds in boiling salted water, then drain and refresh in iced water. Drain again and set aside.

3 Chop the broccoli florets and leaves into smallish pieces, discarding any thick stems. Melt the butter in a large frying pan or wok, add the broccoli and stir-fry for 2 minutes. Sprinkle in 2–3 tablespoons of hot water and stir-fry for another 1–2 minutes until tender. Remove from the heat and season well with the paprika and some salt and pepper. Put to one side.

4 Peel and dice the remaining courgettes, and liquidise with the cream. Season with pepper and grated nutmeg, then set aside.

5 To assemble the gratins, butter four 7.5cm (3 in) metal cooking rings. Cut out and butter 4 squares of greaseproof paper, a little larger than the rings, and place them on a baking sheet. Put the rings on top of the paper. Line the base and sides of the rings with the blanched courgettes, ensuring there are no gaps. Add the broccoli, pressing down into the rings. Cover with the puréed courgette, filling the rings to the top. Smooth with a palette knife.

6 Cook the gratins under a hot grill for about 7–8 minutes, until they are heated through and the top just starts to colour.

7 Meanwhile, make the sauce. Put the wine, vinegar and Chartreuse in a saucepan and simmer until reduced by two thirds. Gradually whisk in 65g (2½oz) of the butter until smooth and glossy. Season to taste and keep warm.

8 Melt the remaining butter and use to brush the fish fillets, then season with salt and pepper. Heat a large, heavy-based frying pan, add the fillets, skin-side down, and fry over a moderate heat for about 3 minutes, until the fish just begins to go opaque.

9 Transfer the fillets to 4 warmed serving plates. Carefully invert the gratins on to the plates. Drizzle the Chartreuse butter sauce over the fish and garnish with the salmon roe, if using, and chervil. Serve immediately, with the sautéed potatoes.

'I'm very competitive and I give everything I do one hundred per cent. That's why I'm here.'
Christopher Souto, Contestant

Duo of Seared Salmon and Scallops

Scallops are one of the great ingredients in the modern culinary repertoire. Beautifully plump and available most of the year, they are now cultivated in Scottish lochs, and my goodness they taste fantastic! The difficulty with scallops is that they are rich and need a contrasting flavour to help them on their way – here a simple sauce of lemon juice and chives does the job.

- → 450G (1LB) SMALL NEW POTATOES
- → 100G (4OZ) UNSALTED BUTTER
- → 2 TBSP CRÈME FRAÎCHE
- → 250G (9OZ) BABY SPINACH
- → 4 X 150G (5OZ) SALMON FILLETS, SKIN ON
- → 2 TBSP OLIVE OIL
- → 200G (7OZ) BABY ASPARAGUS SPEARS
- → A LITTLE VEGETABLE OIL FOR BRUSHING
- → 4 LARGE SCALLOPS
- → JUICE OF ½ LEMON
- → 2 TBSP SNIPPED CHIVES
- → SEA SALT AND FRESHLY GROUND BLACK PEPPER

 MASTERCHEF TOP TIP

Salmon and scallops are a fine combination and work well with spinach and asparagus in this recipe. I would recommend using king scallops, as it is difficult to sear the smaller queen scallops. Eating overcooked scallops is like chewing rubber, so you need a very hot pan in order to cook them quickly. Season the scallops with sea salt and cook for 1 minute on each side. Try not to keep them warm any longer than necessary, as they lose their juices very quickly.

I love spinach in any form. Seasoned with salt, freshly ground pepper and a little grated nutmeg, it is just perfect. Bintje potatoes would be ideal to use here. Just make sure they are cooked through but not overcooked.

Peter Richards, Masterchef Mentor

1 Cook the potatoes in boiling salted water until tender, then drain. Roughly crush with a fork and stir in 25g (1oz) of the butter and the crème fraîche. Season to taste and keep warm.

2 Cook the spinach in a saucepan with a tablespoon of water until just wilted. Drain well, stir in a knob of the butter and season to taste. Keep warm.

3 Heat a ridged griddle pan until very hot. Brush the salmon fillets on both sides with the olive oil and season well. Place the salmon on the griddle, skin-side down, and sear until it has taken on a good golden colour underneath. Turn the fillets over and cook until lightly browned. Remove from the pan and keep warm.

4 Sear the asparagus spears on the hot griddle for 2–3 minutes, until tender and slightly coloured. Remove and keep warm.

5 Lightly brush a heavy-based frying pan with a little vegetable oil and place it over a high heat until very hot. Season the scallops with a little salt, place them in the hot pan and sear for 1 minute on each side, until browned and lightly caramelised. Remove from the pan and keep warm.

6 Add 50g (2oz) of the butter to the frying pan, then the lemon juice, and stir well with a wooden spoon to scrape up any residue from the base of the pan. Return the pan to the heat, whisk in the remaining butter and the chives and season to taste.

7 Arrange the seared salmon and scallops on warm serving plates with the vegetables. Drizzle the chive dressing over the fish and serve immediately.

Masterchef Masterclass
John Torode's Mash

Mashed potato must surely be the ultimate comfort food. Really good mash has to be beaten and worked quite hard until it is creamy and peaky but still has the texture of a good floury potato. If possible, buy potatoes that are covered in protective earth and quite fresh out of the ground. As potatoes get older, the starch begins to break down into sugar, so that you end up with a sweetish, sloppy, more cornflour-textured mash. The best varieties to use are large, floury ones such as Maris Piper, Desiree and Golden Wonder.

You can't really make hard and fast rules about the ratio of liquid or butter to potato. You need to take a look at the texture of your cooked potato and feel your way. It also depends on personal taste and how you plan to serve your mash. To cover a fish pie, it needs to be fairly stiff, whereas as an accompaniment to meat or fish you might want a more luxurious mash that is almost a purée.

There are many theories about how to cook mash but here are a few general principles.

→ Cut the peeled potatoes into even-sized chunks, so that they all cook at the same rate.

→ Put the potatoes in a pan of cold water and bring to the boil, rather than adding them to boiling water; this way, they are less likely to break up.

→ After draining the cooked potatoes, let them steam over the heat for a few minutes so the moisture evaporates.

→ Mash the potatoes until they are smooth and lump-free, then beat them vigorously to give them a light, fluffy texture. Don't use a food processor for this, though, as it makes them gluey.

→ Always serve mashed potato piping hot.

John Torode's
Basic Mash

SERVES 4–6
→ 2KG (4¹/₂LB) FLOURY POTATOES
→ ABOUT 100G (4OZ) BUTTER
→ ABOUT 200ML (7FL OZ) HOT MILK
→ 100ML (3¹/₂FL OZ) DOUBLE CREAM
  (OPTIONAL)
→ SEA SALT AND WHITE PEPPER

1 Peel the potatoes and cut them into even-sized chunks. Place them in a large pan of cold water, add a good handful of sea salt and bring to the boil.

2 Reduce the heat to a gentle simmer, so the water is just moving. Cook until you can easily slip a knife through a potato.

3 Drain the potatoes well in a sieve or colander, then return them to the pan. Place over a very low heat for a minute or two, shaking the pan occasionally, to steam off the excess moisture.

4 Mash with a potato masher or a fork (I prefer a fork). Alternatively pass the potatoes through a potato ricer or sieve. Keep the pan on the heat to evaporate any more moisture that comes from the potatoes as they are mashed.

5 Season well, add the butter and mix it in roughly. Then raise the heat a little and gradually add the milk, beating constantly with a wooden spoon. Work the potato, still on the hob, adding more milk and butter as you like, until the mixture becomes volcanic and starts erupting in bubbles. Add the cream, if using, then taste and adjust the seasoning.

6 Serve straight away, with something equally simple and equally sublime, such as a good piece of roast cod.

Fish Pie with Green Beans

There are fish pies and then there are fish pies! The important thing is that the pie should be moreish and comforting as well as being seasoned on all levels. Often people don't get the proportions correct, such as the ratio of mashed potato to sauce to fish. Many fish pies are made too heavy by the inclusion of a flour-based sauce, but not this one. This recipe could be renamed very, very good fish pie!

→ 675G (1½LB) FLOURY POTATOES, SUCH AS MARIS PIPER, PEELED AND CUT INTO CHUNKS
→ 40G (1½OZ) BUTTER
→ 350ML (12FL OZ) DOUBLE CREAM
→ 2 TBSP OLIVE OIL
→ 1 ONION, FINELY CHOPPED
→ 175G (6OZ) MATURE CHEDDAR CHEESE, GRATED
→ 1 HEAPED TSP MUSTARD POWDER
→ 2–3 TBSP CHOPPED PARSLEY
→ 2 TBSP LEMON JUICE
→ 450G (1LB) THICK SKINLESS COD FILLET
→ 16 RAW TIGER PRAWNS, PEELED
→ 175G (6OZ) FINE GREEN BEANS, TRIMMED
→ SALT AND WHITE PEPPER

1 Preheat the oven to 200°C/400°F/Gas Mark 6.

2 Cook the potatoes in boiling salted water until tender, then drain. Mash well and stir in half the butter and 3 tablespoons of the cream. Season to taste.

3 Heat the remaining butter and half the oil in a small saucepan. Add the onion and fry until soft and translucent. Stir in the remaining cream and bring to the boil, then remove from the heat. Stir in the cheese, mustard, parsley and lemon juice.

4 Slice the cod into meaty chunks and arrange them in a pan in a single layer. Add 100ml (3½fl oz) water, bring to a simmer, then cover and cook for 2–3 minutes, to firm up the fish. Drain well and arrange in an ovenproof serving dish with the prawns.

5 Pour the sauce over the fish. Spoon the potato on top and bake for 30 minutes, until piping hot and golden brown.

6 Put the green beans in a shallow ovenproof dish, coat with the remaining olive oil and season. Bake in the oven with the fish pie for the last 8–10 minutes of cooking time. Drain the oil from the beans and serve them with the fish pie.

Inspired by contestant David Herbert

Mediterranean Cod Fillet with Puy Lentils and Spinach

Lentils always work well with a moist fish such as cod. In fact, this recipe would also be successful with a stronger fish, like sea bass. Small Puy lentils are used here because they cook quickly and do not need soaking first. Remember that lentils will absorb any flavour you throw at them and they do need to be seasoned well. However, never add salt to the cooking water or the lentils will be tough and horrid.

→ 200G (7OZ) PUY LENTILS
→ 4 X 150G (5OZ) PIECES OF THICK COD FILLET, SKINNED
→ 4 TBSP GOOD-QUALITY OLIVE OIL
→ 200G (7OZ) CHORIZO SAUSAGE, THINLY SLICED
→ 1 TBSP LEMON JUICE
→ 225G (8OZ) BABY SPINACH
→ 4 TBSP CHOPPED BASIL
→ 1½ TSP CHOPPED SAGE
→ 1 TBSP CHOPPED MARJORAM
→ SALT AND FRESHLY GROUND BLACK PEPPER

 MASTERCHEF TOP TIP
Where would our chippies be without cod? It's northern Europe's favourite fish. Many people turn away from cod these days, concerned by press reports of diminishing stocks. However, there is now some serious legislation in place concerning cod fishing. Cod are prodigious breeders and, left alone for a short time, their numbers will swell dramatically.

When buying fish, it's preferable to see the whole fish, so you can check for freshness. First, the gills should be bright red. Next, check the eyes, which should be prominent – as the fish ages, the eyes sink. Finally, get your nose right next to it and have a good sniff. Fish should smell of the sea and not of fish!

Most of us buy fillets of cod, in which case a good, thick fillet is what you need, with clear, bright skin. The shoulder end is one of the best cuts.
Gregg Wallace, Masterchef Judge

1 Preheat the oven to 200°C/400°F/Gas Mark 6.

2 Rinse the lentils well under cold running water, then place them in a large saucepan and cover with plenty of fresh water. Bring to the boil and simmer for 25 minutes or until tender. Drain well. Return the lentils to the pan, cover and set aside.

3 Line a baking tray with greased foil and place the fish on it, skinned-side uppermost. Lightly brush the sides of the fish with 1 tablespoon of the olive oil and season with salt and pepper. Cover the top of each fillet with the chorizo slices, overlapping them to resemble fish scales. Place in the oven and cook for 6–8 minutes, until the fish is opaque and just cooked through.

4 While the fish is cooking, return the lentils to a medium heat. Add the remaining olive oil, season with salt and plenty of pepper and heat through. Stir in the lemon juice, spinach and chopped herbs. Cover and cook until the spinach has wilted, shaking the pan occasionally to prevent sticking.

5 Remove from the heat and stir well. Adjust the seasoning, adding more lemon juice, olive oil or salt and pepper as needed.

6 Divide the lentil and spinach mixture between 4 warm serving plates and top with the cod fillets. Serve immediately.

Inspired by contestant Mark Todd

Cod with Wild Mushrooms and Salsa Verde

Cod is a fantastic fish. It has thick, sumptuous white fillets that should be cooked simply and quickly, seasoned at the very last minute as salt can draw out some of the moisture and make it dry and stringy – in the trade it is called cotton wool!

- → 2 AUBERGINES, SLICED
- → 6 TBSP OLIVE OIL
- → 4 X 150G (5OZ) PIECES OF COD, CUT FROM THE THICK END OF THE LOIN, SKIN ON
- → 2 TBSP PLAIN FLOUR
- → 2 TBSP GROUNDNUT OIL
- → 200G (7OZ) MIXED WILD MUSHROOMS, SLICED IF LARGE
- → SALT AND FRESHLY GROUND BLACK PEPPER

For the salsa verde:
- → 5 TSP OLIVE OIL
- → 50G (2OZ) SHALLOTS, FINELY DICED
- → 1 GARLIC CLOVE, FINELY DICED
- → 80G (3½OZ) GREEN PEPPER, FINELY DICED
- → 80G (3½OZ) COURGETTE, FINELY DICED
- → 1 SPRING ONION, FINELY DICED
- → 80G (3½OZ) CUCUMBER, FINELY DICED
- → 50G (2OZ) BABY SPINACH
- → 15G (½OZ) FLAT-LEAF PARSLEY, CHOPPED
- → 15G (½OZ) CHIVES, CHOPPED
- → 15G (½OZ) TARRAGON LEAVES, CHOPPED
- → 1 TBSP PESTO
- → 1 AVOCADO
- → 1 TSP LEMON JUICE

1 First make the salsa verde. Heat a teaspoon of the olive oil in a small, non-stick frying pan, add the shallots and garlic and fry until translucent. Transfer to a bowl. Repeat the process with the pepper, courgette, spring onion and cucumber, frying each vegetable separately until cooked but still retaining some bite and transferring them to the bowl with the shallots.

2 Put the spinach in a small saucepan with 2 tablespoons of boiling water and place over a high heat for about 30 seconds, until wilted. Remove from the heat and add the herbs. Mix the spinach and herbs to a thick paste in a blender or food processor. Stir into the fried vegetables, add the pesto and season well.

3 Halve, stone and peel the avocado, then chop it roughly. Toss with the lemon juice and add to the salsa. Adjust the seasoning if necessary and set aside.

4 Heat a ridged griddle pan. Brush the sliced aubergines with 4 tablespoons of the olive oil and chargrill on both sides until browned and tender. Remove from the heat and keep warm.

5 Preheat the oven to 200°C/400°F/Gas Mark 6. Season the pieces of cod with salt and pepper and dust lightly with the flour. Heat the remaining olive oil in a large, ovenproof frying pan over a high heat. Add the cod, skin-side down, and fry for about 3 minutes, until the skin is crisp. Transfer to the hot oven and leave for 3–4 minutes, until just cooked through.

6 While the fish is cooking, heat a large frying pan until very hot. Add the groundnut oil and then the mushrooms. Cook for 2–3 minutes, until tender, then remove from the heat and keep warm.

7 Stack the aubergine slices and mushrooms on 4 warm serving plates and place the cod on top. Drizzle some salsa verde around the plate and serve immediately.

Name: Christopher Souto
Age: 33
Occupation: Freelance IT Project Manager.
Place of residence: London
Why did you apply to Masterchef?
I wanted to explore my love of food and see if I had the creativity required to produce great meals.
What do you cook at home and who do you cook for?
Up until recently I didn't cook anything at home except fry-ups and the occasional Sunday roast. Now I will cook anything – fresh pastas, home-made soups, ethnic food, anything... the imagination is the only limit.
I mainly cook for friends and my son.
What is your favourite meal?
I love Indian food. But any meal in good company is fantastic.
What are your aspirations in the world of cooking and food?
I would like to open a restaurant in southern Spain.

Name: Caroline Brewester
Age: 38
Occupation: Stockbroker for the last 15 years.
Place of residence: North London
Why did you apply to Masterchef?
I had taken a year out from broking and I'm interested in doing more food stuff. I saw an advert, and I would love to be a food writer so I thought this would be a way of pursuing that.
What do you cook at home and who do you cook for?
I cook all sorts of things, but most of what I cook has to be ready in about half an hour because of the hours I work, so I'm particularly fond of quick and easy recipes to cook at home: mostly English, Italian and North African food. I still have to learn more about Asian cookery. I cook for my husband, who's both my greatest fan and fiercest critic, and friends as well.
What is your favourite meal?
I'm too greedy to have one favourite!
What are your aspirations in the world of cooking and food?
To be a food writer, to show people it really is possible to cook at home and you don't need to aspire to be a chef to do so. There are really simple recipes you can make to impress your friends and your husband and to be a great home cook.

Name: Mark Todd
Age: 25
Occupation: I work for a publishing house as an advertising sales account manager.
Place of residence: Bath (but I'm from Darlington originally)
Why did you apply to Masterchef?
Because I fancied myself as a good cook! My friends told me to go for it, because I cook for them. It was a Friday afternoon at work, I had nothing better to do, so I filled in the application form.
What do you cook at home and who do you cook for?
I cook for anyone who comes to my house, mainly for my fiancée Esther, but also for dinner parties and when I go home to my family (apart from on Sundays when Mum cooks the roast). I like to experiment with different flavours, different produce.
What is your favourite meal?
Kerala chicken with pilau rice is my signature dish at home. I serve it with homemade tarka dal.
What are your aspirations in the world of cooking and food?
I want to own and run a restaurant. I've always wanted to. I want to be sat at the bar all night, with a glass of red wine, in my own restaurant by the time I'm 30.

Masterchef Masterclass
John Torode's Chips

In the UK 38,000 tonnes of potatoes per week are made into chips – which means that one in every four potatoes ends its life as a chip. Everyone loves them. We guard our own plateful fiercely, slapping would-be chip thieves' hands away with the cry, 'Get off my chips!' So why are they so popular? And what makes the perfect chip?

First of all, it has to be made from the right kind of potato – large, floury ones, such as Desiree, Pentland, Cyprus or Maris Piper. These will all produce chips that are crisp on the outside and fluffy in the centre. The potatoes should be covered with a good layer of protective dirt when you buy them – they keep better this way. They should not have been stored too long before use, otherwise their starch reverts to sugar and you won't get that lovely, fluffy interior. Although we tend not to think of potatoes as a seasonal item any more, the large English varieties are at their best for frying from late autumn to late spring.

Chips come in all shapes and sizes: from wafer-thin crisps and game chips to slender French fries, chunky chip-shop chips and crinkle-cut versions. The basic cooking method is the same for all of them. Here are some pointers for success:

→ Use an electric deep-fat fryer or a large, deep saucepan for frying chips. For safety reasons, never leave it unattended while cooking, and make sure the oil doesn't overheat (an electric fryer has a built-in thermostat; otherwise you can use a thermometer).

→ Before cooking, wash the chips in cold water to remove some of the starch, then dry them thoroughly to prevent splattering when you put them in the hot fat.

→ Use a generous quantity of clean oil and cook the chips in small batches, otherwise when you add the chips to the oil the temperature will drop dramatically, resulting in soggy chips. I recommend 2 litres (3½ pints) of oil to 300g (11oz) potatoes.

→ Fry the chips twice: once at a low temperature to cook them through and ensure tenderness, then again at a higher temperature so they become crisp and golden. This is the method used by chippies and restaurants across the country.

→ Drain the chips well on kitchen paper after frying, so they won't be greasy.

John Torode's
Big Chips

SERVES 4
→ 6 LARGE, FLOURY POTATOES
→ SUNFLOWER OR GROUNDNUT OIL
  FOR DEEP-FRYING
→ SALT

VARIATIONS
→ **French fries**
To make French fries, cut the potatoes into chips 8mm wide and about 5cm long. Soak them in cold water 3 or 4 times, then follow the instructions above, reducing the time for each frying to about 3 minutes.

→ **Crisps**
To make crisps at home, it is useful to have a mandoline or a food processor with a slicing attachment. Peel the potatoes and slice them to credit-card thickness – if you hold a slice up to the light you should almost be able to see through it. Place the slices in a sinkful of cold water and run the water over the top of them, stirring them about until the water is clear. This washes out all the excess starch so they become very crisp. Heat the oil to 190°C/375°F, using 2 litres of oil to 100g (4oz) of crisps. Gently place each slice in the oil as if you were the dealer at a card game. Cook for 3 minutes, stirring occasionally to prevent them sticking together (if they do stick, either the oil isn't hot enough or the potatoes have not been washed of all their starch). Cook for another 6 minutes or so, until they are well browned and crisp, then remove from the oil and place on kitchen paper to drain. Place in a brown paper bag while still warm and sprinkle with salt.

1 Peel the potatoes and cut them into chips 3cm (1¼ in) wide. Fill the sink with cold water, add the chips and leave them to soak for 5 minutes. Change the water and leave for a further 5 minutes. Drain well, then place the chips on a clean tea towel and pat dry.

2 Heat the oil to 140°C/275°F in a deep-fat fryer or a large, deep saucepan. Lower a small batch of chips into the oil in a chip basket and cook for 8–10 minutes, until the chips are soft and flaccid but still pale. Lift the basket out of the oil and drain, then spread the chips out on a tray lined with kitchen paper. Repeat with the remaining chips. This initial frying can be done several hours in advance. Once the chips are cold, you can store them in the fridge, which will make the insides even fluffier.

3 The final frying should be quite quick and the oil must be hot. The quantity of chips in the oil will determine how quickly it returns to the temperature you require so the outside is sealed and begins to brown. Heat the oil to 190°C/375°F and lower a small batch of chips into it. Leave to cook for 2 minutes, then give them a little shake. Cook for a further 4–5 minutes, until they are well coloured and crisp. Remove from the oil and leave to drain for a few minutes, then place in a bowl and sprinkle with salt.

Monkfish in Parma Ham with Chilli Beurre Blanc, Brussels Sprout Purée and Potato Waffles

This is a classic idea given a Masterchef twist with the addition of the punchy chilli beurre blanc. You could call it a new take on fish, chips and mushy peas. Monkfish is a great fish when fresh but if old and tired the flesh can become woolly when cooked, so make sure you buy yours from a good fishmonger.

→ 6–8 SLICES OF PARMA HAM (NOT TOO THIN)
→ 500G (1LB 2OZ) MONKFISH TAIL, DIVIDED INTO 2 FILLETS
→ 25G (1OZ) CLARIFIED BUTTER
→ SALT AND FRESHLY GROUND BLACK PEPPER
For the Brussels sprout purée:
→ 300G (11 OZ) BRUSSELS SPROUTS, TRIMMED AND HALVED
→ 25G (1OZ) BUTTER
→ 4–6 TBSP DOUBLE CREAM
For the potato waffles:
→ 2 LARGE WHITE POTATOES (ABOUT 300G/11OZ EACH), PEELED
→ 1 LITRE (1¾ PINTS) GROUNDNUT OIL
For the chilli beurre blanc:
→ 2 MILD LONG RED CHILLIES
→ 150G (5OZ) BUTTER
→ 20G (¾OZ) SHALLOT, FINELY CHOPPED
→ 1 TBSP WHITE WINE VINEGAR
→ 85ML (3FL OZ) DRY WHITE WINE
→ 85ML (3FL OZ) FISH STOCK
→ 1 TBSP DOUBLE CREAM
→ SALT AND WHITE PEPPER

1 Lay the Parma ham slices on a length of cling film, slightly overlapping them. Season the monkfish fillets with pepper and place them one on top of the other, thin end to thick end, to form an even cylinder. Then place them on the ham and roll up, using the cling film to help. Tuck in the ends of the ham. Wrap tightly in the cling film and chill for 1 hour.

2 Meanwhile, make the sprout purée. Cook the sprouts in boiling salted water for 3–4 minutes, until just tender. Drain well, place in a food processor and blend to a chunky purée. Add the butter, 4 tablespoons of the cream and some pepper. Blend again to purée, adding more cream if necessary for a looser texture. Spoon the purée into a small saucepan and set aside.

3 Cut the potatoes into waffle slices using the waffle attachment of a mandoline. Put them in a large bowl of cold water. Pour the groundnut oil into a large frying pan to a depth of about 6cm (2½ in) and heat to 160°C/325°F.

4 Drain the potato slices, dry them well on kitchen paper and test the oil by dropping a slice of potato into it. It should brown in about a minute. Fry the potato slices in batches, removing them with a slotted spoon when done and leaving to drain on baking trays lined with kitchen paper.

5 For the chilli sauce, cut the chillies lengthways in half, remove the seeds and set them aside. Finely dice 1 chilli, then roughly chop the other one and set it aside with the chilli seeds.

6 Melt 15g (½oz) of the butter in a small, heavy-based saucepan (dice the remaining butter and chill it). Add the shallot to the pan

and fry gently until translucent. Add the chilli seeds, roughly chopped chilli and the white wine vinegar. Simmer until reduced by two-thirds. Pour in the white wine and reduce again by two-thirds, then add the fish stock and reduce by two-thirds a final time. Strain the reduction into a clean saucepan and set aside.

7 To cook the fish, preheat the oven to 200°C/400°F/Gas Mark 6. Heat a heavy-based non-stick frying pan until very hot and add the clarified butter. Remove the cling film from the fish and brown it on all sides in the butter. Transfer to a baking sheet lined with baking parchment and bake for 8–10 minutes. Remove from the oven and leave to rest in a warm place for 6–7 minutes.

8 To finish the sauce, reheat the reduction in the pan, then stir in the cream. Whisk in the chilled diced butter a little at a time over a medium heat. Season to taste with salt and white pepper, then stir in the finely diced chilli.

9 Just before serving, gently reheat the Brussels sprout purée. Place the trays of potato waffles in the oven for a couple of minutes to heat through and crisp up, then sprinkle them with a little salt.

10 Slice the monkfish into 4 and put it on to 4 warmed plates with a spoonful of the Brussels sprout purée and a pile of waffles. Drizzle a little of the chilli beurre blanc over the fish and serve the rest separately.

Marinated Seared Tuna on a Garlic and Anchovy Croûton with Creamed Fennel and French Beans Provençal

Katherine's inspired recipe evokes the flavours of the Mediterranean. The tuna, anchovies and beans immediately suggest a classic salad niçoise, but the creamy fennel adds a different texture, binding the dish into a coherent whole.

- → 4 X 175G (6OZ) TUNA STEAKS, ABOUT 2.5CM (1 IN) THICK
- → 100ML (3½FL OZ) WHITE WINE
- → 15G (½OZ) BUTTER
- → 1 FENNEL BULB, THINLY SLICED
- → OLIVE OIL FOR BRUSHING
- → SALT AND FRESHLY GROUND BLACK PEPPER

For the marinade:
- → 1 TSP FENNEL SEEDS
- → JUICE OF 1 LIME
- → 2 TBSP LIGHT SOY SAUCE
- → 1 TBSP OLIVE OIL

For the garlic and anchovy croûtons:
- → 2 TBSP OLIVE OIL
- → 75G (3OZ) BUTTER
- → 4 SLICES OF GOOD-QUALITY WHITE BREAD
- → 4 ANCHOVY FILLETS IN OLIVE OIL
- → 3 GARLIC CLOVES, CRUSHED

For the French beans Provençal:
- → 150G (5OZ) FRENCH BEANS, TRIMMED
- → 1 TBSP OLIVE OIL
- → 1 GARLIC CLOVE, CRUSHED
- → 2 TBSP TOMATO PURÉE
- → ½ TSP VERJUICE
- → 2–3 SUN-DRIED TOMATOES IN OLIVE OIL, FINELY CHOPPED
- → ½ RED PEPPER, ROASTED, PEELED AND FINELY SLICED
- → 50G (2OZ) GREEN OLIVES, SLICED

Ⓜ MASTERCHEF TOP TIP

Verjuice – or verjus, to give it its French name – is the juice of unripe white grapes and has a fresh but acidic taste. You only need a small amount, so use it judiciously.
Peter Richards, Masterchef Mentor

1 Mix all the marinade ingredients together in a shallow, non-metallic dish and season to taste. Lay the tuna in the dish and turn until thoroughly coated in the marinade.

2 For the fennel, bring the wine and butter to the boil in a small pan. Add the fennel and some seasoning and cook over a medium heat for 15 minutes, until the fennel is soft and creamy and the liquid has evaporated. Remove from the heat and keep warm.

3 For the croûtons, heat half the olive oil and butter in a large frying pan, add 2 slices of bread and fry until golden on both sides. Remove from the pan and repeat with the remaining bread, oil and butter. Cut off the crusts to make pieces a similar size to the tuna steaks. Place on kitchen paper to absorb excess oil. Dry the anchovy fillets on kitchen paper and mash with the garlic to make a paste. Spread the paste over the fried bread and set aside.

4 For the French beans, bring a saucepan of lightly salted water to the boil and cook the beans for 3–4 minutes, until just tender. Drain, then cool under cold running water. Warm the olive oil in a pan and add the garlic. Cook for a few seconds, then add the tomato purée, verjuice and some salt and pepper. Cook gently for 2–3 minutes, then stir in the sun-dried tomatoes, red pepper, olives and green beans. Warm through, then set aside.

5 Preheat the oven to 190°C/375°F/Gas Mark 5. Heat a ridged griddle pan and brush with oil. Wipe the tuna dry on kitchen paper and brush with a little olive oil. Lay the tuna on the hot griddle and sear for about 2–3 minutes on each side, until lightly caramelised on the outside but still pink in the middle. While the tuna is cooking, put the croûtons in the oven to warm through.

6 Put a croûton on each serving plate. Top with a tuna steak and some creamed fennel and serve with the French beans.

Inspired by contestant Melanie Bullard

Sea Bass with Anchovy Sauce, Spinach and Cannellini Beans

The River Café in London has been using the combination of sea bass and anchovies for as long as I can remember. The anchovies provide the saltiness that is needed to make the sea bass stand out as one of the greatest all-round fish. Bolstered by pancetta and cannellini beans, this will make a great addition to your winter repertoire.

→ 100G (4OZ) PANCETTA, FINELY DICED
→ 400G (14OZ) TIN OF CANNELLINI BEANS, DRAINED AND RINSED
→ 2 HEAPED TBSP FINELY CHOPPED FLAT-LEAF PARSLEY
→ 1 TBSP FINELY CHOPPED MINT
→ 3 GARLIC CLOVES, FINELY CHOPPED
→ JUICE OF 1 LEMON
→ 2–3 TBSP OLIVE OIL
→ 2 TBSP PLAIN FLOUR
→ 1 TSP SEA SALT
→ 4 X 200G (7OZ) SEA BASS FILLETS, SKIN ON
→ 50G (2OZ) BUTTER
→ 200G (7OZ) BABY SPINACH
→ 5 ANCHOVY FILLETS IN EXTRA VIRGIN OLIVE OIL, FINELY CHOPPED, PLUS 2 TSP OF THEIR OIL
→ 1 TSP CHOPPED THYME
→ 4 TBSP DRY SHERRY
→ FRESHLY GROUND BLACK PEPPER

1 Preheat the oven to 200°C/400°F/Gas Mark 6.

2 In a frying pan, slowly cook the pancetta until it is beginning to crisp up. Stir in the cannellini beans and heat through. Add the parsley, mint, half the garlic and the lemon juice. Season with plenty of black pepper and drizzle a little of the olive oil over the top, then cover and keep warm.

3 Mix the flour and sea salt together on a plate and lightly dust the skin side of the fish fillets, tapping off any excess flour.

4 Heat a little of the olive oil in a large ovenproof frying pan. Place the fillets in the pan, skin-side down, and cook over a high heat for 5 minutes to crisp the skin. Transfer the pan to the oven and cook for 4–5 minutes, until the fish is just done. Do not turn the fish over.

5 Put half the butter in a saucepan with 1 tablespoon of water and bring to the boil. Stir in the spinach, then cover the pan and cook for 1 minute, until the spinach has wilted. Remove from the heat and keep warm. Drain off any excess liquid before serving.

6 In a small saucepan, heat the 2 teaspoons of anchovy oil, add the remaining garlic and the anchovies and cook over a low heat, stirring, for about 2 minutes, until the garlic is soft. Add the thyme and sherry and warm through. Remove from the heat and whisk in the remaining butter.

7 Pile up the spinach in the centre of 4 warm serving plates. Place the fish fillets on top of the spinach. Spoon the pancetta and beans around the outside and drizzle the anchovy sauce over the fish. Serve immediately.

Inspired by contestant Henry Mackley

Sea Bass with Fennel and Red Onion en Papillote served with Butter Bean and Tarragon Mash

The term *en papillote* simply means baked in a paper or foil wrapping. When the dish is taken from the oven, it should be presented at the table with a sharp knife to open the parcel and release the steam, which will be richly scented by the fennel. This heady mix helps to stimulate the appetite.

The butter bean mash can dry out very quickly, so if possible add a little hot stock or water just before serving.

→ 1 RED ONION, FINELY SLICED
→ 1 FENNEL BULB, FINELY SLICED
→ 1 LEMON, FINELY SLICED
→ 4 SMALL SPRIGS OF TARRAGON
→ 3 TBSP EXTRA VIRGIN OLIVE OIL
→ 4 X 150G (5OZ) SEA BASS FILLETS, SKIN ON
→ 60ML (2FL OZ) DRY WHITE WINE
→ SALT AND FRESHLY GROUND BLACK PEPPER
For the butter bean and tarragon mash:
→ 340G (12OZ) DRIED BUTTER BEANS, SOAKED IN COLD WATER OVERNIGHT
→ 3 TBSP OLIVE OIL
→ 2 SHALLOTS, FINELY CHOPPED
→ 350ML (12FL OZ) CHICKEN STOCK
→ 2 TSP CHOPPED TARRAGON
→ 1 TBSP LEMON JUICE

Ⓜ **MASTERCHEF TOP TIP**

Fish is my favourite form of protein, with so many interesting flavours and textures, but there are pitfalls. Be careful when using something like fennel with sea bass. It has a very strong flavour, unlike the sea bass, which has a delicate taste that needs drawing out. The combination of ingredients in this dish does the sea bass proud. Do not overcook the fish.

Wild sea bass is very expensive and is in danger of being overfished, so use it wisely. Farmed sea bass is now widely available. Although the flavour and texture aren't quite as good as the wild fish, it is fine for this recipe.

Peter Richards, Masterchef Mentor

1 First make the bean mash. Drain and rinse the soaked beans, then put them in a large pan and cover with fresh water. Bring to the boil and boil rapidly for 10 minutes. Reduce the heat, cover and simmer for 40 minutes or until the beans are tender. Drain and set aside.

2 Heat 1 tablespoon of the olive oil in a medium-sized saucepan, add the shallots and cook over a moderate heat until soft and translucent. Add the beans and the chicken stock. Bring to the boil, then reduce the heat and simmer, uncovered, for about 15 minutes, until most of the liquid has been absorbed. Remove from the heat.

3 Stir in the remaining olive oil. Roughly mash the beans with a fork, then stir in the tarragon and lemon juice and season well. Transfer to a serving dish and keep warm.

4 For the sea bass, preheat the oven to 220°C/425°F/Gas Mark 7. Spread a large sheet of aluminium foil out on a baking tray, letting it overlap the edges. Layer the red onion, fennel and lemon slices in the middle. Add the tarragon and olive oil and season well.

5 Lay the sea bass fillets, skin-side up, on top of the vegetables. Pull up the edges of the foil and pour in the wine. Pull the edges of the foil together and seal tightly. Bake for 12–15 minutes.

6 Transfer the foil parcel to a large plate and slit it open at the table. Serve with the butter bean mash.

John Dory and Scallops with Salsa Verde

John Dory and scallops are both quite meaty, as they have a good, solid texture when cooked and go well with a flavourful sauce such as salsa verde. Remember to have the frying pan nice and hot before adding the John Dory, because if it is placed in a cold pan it will braise instead of fry and not have a very pleasant texture.

→ 400G (14OZ) LA RATTE POTATOES OR OTHER SMALL SALAD POTATOES
→ 200G (7OZ) PURPLE SPROUTING BROCCOLI
→ 4 X 150G (5OZ) JOHN DORY FILLETS, SKINNED
→ 6 LARGE SCALLOPS
→ 25G (1OZ) BUTTER
→ SALT AND FRESHLY GROUND BLACK PEPPER

For the salsa verde:
→ 4 ANCHOVY FILLETS IN EXTRA VIRGIN OLIVE OIL, DRAINED
→ 2 TSP GOOD-QUALITY CAPERS IN SHERRY VINEGAR, DRAINED
→ 1 GARLIC CLOVE, FINELY CHOPPED
→ 4 TBSP FINELY CHOPPED FLAT-LEAF PARSLEY
→ 2 TBSP FINELY CHOPPED TARRAGON
→ 3 TBSP EXTRA VIRGIN OLIVE OIL

For the caramelised lemon slices:
→ A SMALL KNOB OF BUTTER
→ 4 LEMON SLICES

1 Steam the potatoes and purple sprouting broccoli until tender.

2 Meanwhile, make the salsa verde. Finely chop the anchovy fillets and capers, then put them in a pestle and mortar. Add the garlic and pound to a paste. Stir in the parsley, tarragon and extra virgin olive oil, then set aside.

3 For the lemon slices, melt the butter in a small, non-stick frying pan over a fairly high heat. Add the lemon slices and sear for 30 seconds on each side, until tinged with brown. Remove from the pan and set aside.

4 Season the John Dory fillets and the scallops with salt and pepper. Melt the butter in a large, non-stick frying pan, add the fish fillets and scallops and fry very quickly on both sides; they will take about 2–3 minutes in total, depending on size. Remove the scallops from the pan and slice them horizontally in half.

5 Arrange the steamed vegetables, John Dory and scallops on 4 warmed plates. Drizzle a little salsa verde over the fish and garnish with the lemon slices. Serve immediately, accompanied by the remaining salsa verde.

'I've cooked all my life, since I was six. Cooking is second nature to me – I do it almost as easily as breathing.'
Thomasina Miers, Contestant

Meat, Poultry and Game

Inspired by contestant Caroline Brewester

Chicken Breasts with Wild Mushroom and Marsala Sauce and Potato Gratin

Most people are guilty of overcooking a chicken breast at some time or another, turning it into a dry, unpalatable lump. Here, Caroline has come up with a cooking method that prevents the delicate breasts from drying out – very clever indeed.

- → 2 TBSP CLARIFIED BUTTER
- → 4 CHICKEN BREASTS, SKIN ON
- → 1 ONION, THINLY SLICED
- → 1 CARROT, THINLY SLICED
- → SALT AND FRESHLY
  GROUND BLACK PEPPER

For the potato gratin:
- → 4 POTATOES, PEELED AND FINELY SLICED
- → 3 GARLIC CLOVES, PEELED
- → 150ML (1/4 PINT) DOUBLE CREAM
- → ABOUT 250ML (8FL OZ) MILK
- → 15G (1/2OZ) PARMESAN CHEESE,
  FRESHLY GRATED

For the sauce:
- → 150G (5OZ) MIXED WILD MUSHROOMS
- → 3 SHALLOTS, FINELY CHOPPED
- → 250ML (8FL OZ) DRY MARSALA
- → 300ML (1/2 PINT) BROWN CHICKEN STOCK
- → A KNOB OF COLD BUTTER

MASTERCHEF TOP TIP

Caroline showed us a little trick she learned from Bill Granger, the great Australian chef with a flair for making good food look simple. By placing a strip of paper the length of a ruler in the bottom of each muffin cup so the ends of the paper stand up proud, then filling the muffin cups with the potato mixture, you can use the paper like handles to lift out each cooked potato stack. Smart thinking!

John Torode, Masterchef Judge

1 Preheat the oven to 200°C/400°F/Gas Mark 6.

2 Heat the clarified butter in a large frying pan, add the chicken breasts, skin-side down, and fry until crisp and golden brown. Remove from the heat.

3 Put the onion and carrot slices in a small roasting tin, then put the chicken breasts on top, skin-side up. Season with salt and pepper and add enough water just to reach the bottom of the chicken breasts. Roast for 20–30 minutes, until the chicken is cooked through. Remove from the oven and leave to rest for 5 minutes (the onion and carrot can be discarded).

4 For the potato gratin, grease 4 cups of a deep muffin tin. Rinse the sliced potatoes in a colander under cold water, then transfer to a large saucepan. Bruise the garlic cloves and add to the pan. Pour in the double cream and enough milk just to cover the potatoes, then season. Bring to the boil, then reduce the heat and simmer for 5 minutes, until the potatoes begin to soften. Remove from the heat. Spoon the mixture into the greased muffin cups and sprinkle the Parmesan cheese on top. Bake for 10–15 minutes, until the top is golden brown and the potatoes are tender. Keep warm.

5 For the sauce, briefly fry the mushrooms in the pan in which the chicken was cooked. Remove with a slotted spoon and set aside. Stir the shallots into the pan and fry gently until soft and translucent. Add the marsala, bring to the boil and simmer until reduced by half. Stir in the stock and simmer until reduced by half again. Pour in any juices from the cooked chicken, then whisk in the butter and season to taste. Stir the mushrooms into the sauce and reheat gently.

6 Carefully lift the gratins out of their cups and place on 4 warm plates. Slice the chicken breasts and arrange on the plates. Spoon the mushroom sauce around the chicken and serve immediately.

Chicken Breasts with Tarragon Sauce and Baby Carrots

Shel chose a simple, classic dish here. It is full of flavour and surprisingly addictive. Try serving it with some good mashed potato.

→ 4 SKINLESS, BONELESS CHICKEN BREASTS
→ 2 TBSP PLAIN FLOUR
→ 4 SPRIGS OF TARRAGON
→ 25G (1OZ) BUTTER
→ 1½ TBSP SUNFLOWER OIL
→ 2 SHALLOTS, FINELY CHOPPED
→ 250ML (8FL OZ) DRY WHITE WINE
→ 350ML (12FL OZ) CHICKEN STOCK
→ 4 TBSP CRÈME FRAÎCHE
→ 16 BABY CARROTS, SCRUBBED CLEAN
→ SALT AND FRESHLY GROUND
   BLACK PEPPER

1 Pat the chicken dry with kitchen paper. Season the flour with salt and pepper and dust the chicken breasts with it.

2 Set aside 2 tarragon sprigs for garnish. Remove the leaves from the remaining sprigs and chop them coarsely.

3 Heat half the butter and 1 tablespoon of the oil in a large, heavy-based frying pan over a moderate heat. Add the chicken breasts and fry for 6–7 minutes on each side, until cooked through. Remove from the pan, cover and keep warm.

4 Add the shallots to the pan with the rest of the oil and fry over a medium heat until translucent. Add the wine and half the chopped tarragon. Boil until the wine has reduced by half, scraping the bottom of the pan to dislodge any sediment. Add the chicken stock and reduce by half again.

5 Stir in the crème fraîche and the remaining chopped tarragon, then return the chicken to the pan to warm through for about a minute on each side. Taste and adjust the seasoning.

6 Place the carrots in a heavy-based pan with the remaining butter and 100ml (3½fl oz) water. Season with salt and pepper, then bring to the boil over a high heat and cook for 3–4 minutes.

7 Remove from the heat and leave the carrots in the liquor for about 2 minutes to complete the cooking. Drain well, then serve with the chicken and tarragon sauce.

Stuffed Chicken Parma Parcels

When Scott made these parcels he said that he wanted them to resemble little hams, and strangely enough they do! The boned chicken legs must have the skin removed or the ham will not stick to the meat. Use good-quality dried porcini mushrooms for the best flavour and make sure they are reconstituted properly, as they can be tough if not allowed to soak for long enough.

→ 4 CHICKEN LEGS, SKINNED AND BONED
→ 50G (2OZ) DRIED PORCINI MUSHROOMS
→ 2 SHALLOTS, FINELY CHOPPED
→ 50G (2OZ) BUTTER
→ 2 GARLIC CLOVES, CRUSHED
→ 150G (5OZ) BABY SPINACH
→ 100G (4OZ) MOZZARELLA CHEESE, GRATED
→ 250G (9OZ) RICOTTA CHEESE
→ 8 SLICES OF PARMA HAM
→ 3 TBSP OLIVE OIL
→ 1 TSP BALSAMIC VINEGAR
→ SALT AND FRESHLY GROUND BLACK PEPPER

ⓜ MASTERCHEF TOP TIP

Boning a chicken leg is not difficult. Just follow the line of the bone with the tip of a sharp boning knife, gently scraping the meat away as you go. Remember that chicken bones are brittle. It is best to cut through the joints rather than chopping through bones, as they will chip and splinter.

Peter Richards, Masterchef Mentor

1 Preheat the oven to 200°C/400°F/Gas Mark 6.

2 Place the chicken meat between 2 layers of cling film. Flatten to an even thickness with a meat mallet or rolling pin, then set aside.

3 Put the dried porcini in a bowl and pour on 250ml (8fl oz) hot water. Leave for 30 minutes, then drain well, reserving the soaking liquor. Slice the mushrooms if large.

4 Fry the shallots in the butter until soft and translucent. Add the porcini and garlic and cook for 2 minutes. Stir in the spinach and cook until wilted. Remove from the heat and drain off any excess liquid.

5 Mix the grated mozzarella and ricotta together in a bowl and stir in the spinach mixture. Season to taste.

6 Lay 2 slices of Parma ham on a board, slightly overlapping. Place a flattened chicken leg on top. Spoon a quarter of the stuffing mixture into the middle of the leg and roll it up, with the Parma ham on the outside. Secure with a cocktail stick. Repeat with the remaining chicken legs. Chill for 30 minutes.

7 Heat the oil in an ovenproof frying pan and brown the stuffed chicken legs for 2–3 minutes on each side. Transfer the pan to the oven and cook, uncovered, for 20 minutes or until golden brown and cooked through. Remove from the oven and transfer the chicken to a plate, removing the cocktail sticks. Keep warm.

8 Pour the reserved porcini liquor into the pan and bring to the boil on the hob, scraping up any residue from the base of the pan with a wooden spoon. Simmer until reduced by half, then add the balsamic vinegar and cook for 1–2 minutes. Serve with the chicken.

Thai Green Chicken Curry

A well-made green curry is a wonderful thing. It needs punch but, more importantly, it also needs heat. After you've been handling chillies, remember to wash your hands – first in cold water, then with soap. If you use hot water first, you will open the pores and end up with painful hands.

→ 150ML (¼ PINT) COCONUT CREAM
→ 8 SKINLESS CHICKEN THIGHS, BONED AND CUT INTO 2CM (¾ IN) DICE
→ 400ML (14FL OZ) TIN OF COCONUT MILK
→ 2 KAFFIR LIME LEAVES
→ 1½ TBSP THAI FISH SAUCE (*NAM PLA*)
→ 1 TSP SUGAR
→ 150G (5OZ) AUBERGINE, CUT INTO BITE-SIZED PIECES
→ A HANDFUL OF BASIL LEAVES

For the green curry paste:
→ 1 TBSP CORIANDER SEEDS
→ 1 TSP CUMIN SEEDS
→ 15 GREEN BIRD'S EYE CHILLIES, CHOPPED
→ 3 TBSP FINELY CHOPPED SHALLOTS
→ 1 TBSP FINELY CHOPPED GARLIC
→ 1 TSP FINELY CHOPPED GALANGAL
→ 1 TBSP FINELY SLICED LEMONGRASS
→ 1 TSP FINELY CHOPPED KAFFIR LIME LEAVES
→ ½ TSP FINELY CHOPPED CORIANDER ROOT
→ 5 BLACK PEPPERCORNS
→ 1 TSP SALT
→ 1 TSP SHRIMP PASTE

1 For the curry paste, dry-fry the coriander and cumin seeds in a wok over a low heat for about 5 minutes, then grind to a powder in a pestle and mortar.

2 Put all the rest of the curry paste ingredients except the shrimp paste into a food processor and mix well. Add the ground roasted spices and the shrimp paste and blend to a fine-textured paste.

3 For the curry, heat the coconut cream in a wok until it begins to have an oily sheen. Add 3 level tablespoons of the green curry paste and stir well (the rest of the paste will keep in the fridge for about a week, or it can be frozen). Stir in the chicken and cook until it begins to brown.

4 Add the coconut milk, lime leaves, fish sauce and sugar and bring to the boil. Add the aubergine and simmer for about 20 minutes, until the chicken is cooked through.

5 Stir in the basil leaves. Remove from the heat and serve with fragrant jasmine rice or noodles.

 MASTERCHEF TOP TIP
To make authentic Thai dishes, you need to get hold of genuine Thai ingredients. Nowadays most big cities have a Thai emporium, thanks to the rise in popularity of Thai restaurants. They usually have fresh imports delivered once or twice a week. Ask at your nearest Thai shop which days their produce arrives, and shop then.
Gregg Wallace, Masterchef Judge

Masterchef Masterclass
John Torode's coating and crumbing

I have always enjoyed food that has been cooked in some form of casing, whether it is breadcrumbs, egg or batter. There are several advantages. First, a delicate piece of fish, meat or even vegetable is well protected in this way, allowing it to be subject to high heat and cooked quickly. Secondly, the food remains tender and retains all its juices. And finally, you can use a more expensive cut without it losing volume during cooking, thus making it go further.

The principle is simple: the protective casing seals quickly when heat is applied, allowing the interior to steam. This reduces loss from evaporation and at the same time retains all the flavour and nutrients.

Below are some general guidelines for coating food before frying:
→ The pieces of food should be an even thickness. If coating uneven cuts of meat, such as chicken breasts, put them between two sheets of cling film and bat them out with a meat mallet or rolling pin.
→ Season your coating ingredients well with salt and pepper, plus any other flavourings you like, such as herbs, spices or cheese.
→ Coatings usually consist of flour, then beaten egg, and sometimes a final layer of breadcrumbs. Use just a light dusting of flour, then dip the food in the egg until thoroughly coated and let the excess drain off.
→ If adding a coating of breadcrumbs, spread these out in a shallow dish and press the food in them gently so it is covered in a thin, even layer. Then turn it over to coat the other side.
→ Shallow-fry the coated food in a generous amount of oil or butter, but not so much that the food is swimming in it.
→ Make sure the fat is sizzling hot (but not smoking hot) before adding the food. If it isn't hot enough, the coating will not seal quickly enough and will be soggy. If it is too hot, the coating will burn.

John Torode's
Veal Escalopes Coated with Egg and Parmesan

SERVES 4

→ 4 VEAL ESCALOPES, WEIGHING ABOUT 120G (4½OZ) EACH
→ 50G (2OZ) ROCKET
→ 4 TBSP OLIVE OIL
→ 4 TBSP VEGETABLE OIL
→ 50G (2OZ) PLAIN FLOUR
→ 50G (2OZ) BUTTER
→ 2 TSP WHITE WINE VINEGAR
→ FRESHLY GROUND BLACK PEPPER
→ 1 LEMON, QUARTERED, TO SERVE

For the coating:

→ 2 MEDIUM EGGS
→ 4 ANCHOVIES, FINELY CHOPPED
→ 175G (6OZ) PARMESAN CHEESE, FRESHLY GRATED
→ 2 TBSP CHOPPED FLAT-LEAF PARSLEY
→ ½ TSP FRESHLY GROUND BLACK PEPPER

Dipped in a light coating of egg and cheese, the veal in this recipe is substantial enough to be served with just some rocket salad to accompany it. It makes a good winter lunch or supper dish. Pork fillets can be used instead of veal.

1 Put the veal escalopes between 2 sheets of cling film and bat them out with a meat mallet or a rolling pin to about 1 cm (½ in) thick.

2 For the coating, put the eggs in a large bowl and whisk together for 1 minute, until light. Stir in the anchovies, Parmesan, parsley and black pepper.

3 Place the rocket in a shallow serving dish and dress with the olive oil and some black pepper, then set aside.

4 Heat a large, heavy-based frying pan over a high heat and add the vegetable oil.

5 Spread the flour out in a large, shallow dish and turn the veal escalopes in it until evenly coated. Then dip them in the egg mixture. Place the escalopes in the pan and cook for 1 minute. Reduce the heat to medium and cook for a further 2 minutes, until golden underneath.

6 Turn and cook the other side for 2–3 minutes, then add the butter to the pan. When it has melted, pour in the vinegar, tilting the pan to ensure the juices combine.

7 Remove the escalopes from the pan and lay them on the dressed rocket. Drizzle with the melted butter from the pan and serve with the lemon wedges.

Inspired by contestant Mark Todd

Coq au Vin

Elizabeth David cooked her chicken whole for coq au vin, then caramelised the onions in butter and sugar and added them at the end. Other people joint their chicken and add the mushrooms for the last few minutes' cooking. I think it's important to use a chicken with quite a bit of fat on it, and don't ruin the texture by overcooking. Alternatively, you can use just the well-flavoured thigh meat, as in this recipe.

→ 3 TBSP OLIVE OIL
→ 100G (4OZ) SMOKED STREAKY BACON, CUT INTO SMALL STRIPS
→ 16 SMALL SHALLOTS, PEELED
→ 8–12 CHICKEN THIGHS
→ 1 CARROT, CUT INTO BATONS
→ 2 CELERY STICKS, CHOPPED
→ 1 SMALL ONION, FINELY CHOPPED
→ 4 TBSP BRANDY
→ 400ML (14FL OZ) GOOD-QUALITY RED WINE
→ 200ML (7FL OZ) CHICKEN STOCK
→ 1 BOUQUET GARNI, MADE UP OF 3 SPRIGS OF THYME, 2 BAY LEAVES AND 1 SAGE LEAF
→ 2 GARLIC CLOVES, PEELED
→ 2 TSP CORNFLOUR
→ 150G (5OZ) BUTTON MUSHROOMS

1 Preheat the oven to 190ºC/375ºF/Gas Mark 5.

2 Heat 2 tablespoons of the oil in a large casserole, add the bacon and shallots and fry over a medium heat until lightly coloured. Remove from the pan and set aside.

3 Raise the heat and add the chicken pieces to the pan (cook them in batches if necessary). Sear for about 5 minutes, until browned, then remove from the pan and set aside.

4 Reduce the heat, add the carrot, celery and onion and sweat for 3–4 minutes, until the vegetables are just picking up some colour. Return the chicken to the pan.

5 Pour in the brandy and warm through. Remove from the heat and set it alight with a match, standing well back. After about a minute, cover with a lid to extinguish the flame.

6 Return the pan to the heat and add the wine, stock, bouquet garni and garlic, plus a little water if necessary to cover. Bring to the boil, skim off any foam from the surface and cover with a lid. Place in the oven and cook for 30–40 minutes, until the chicken is tender.

7 Skim off most of the fat released from the chicken. Mix the cornflour to a paste with 2 tablespoons of water and stir it into the cooking juices. Bring to the boil to thicken the juices slightly, then season to taste.

8 Heat the remaining oil in a large frying pan. Reheat the bacon strips and shallots in it, frying until the shallots caramelise. Add the mushrooms and cook for 3 minutes, then season with a little salt and pepper. Mix the bacon, shallots and mushrooms with the chicken and serve.

Inspired by contestant Helen Cristofoli

Pork Wellington with Apple and Sage Compote

Pork Wellington is like beef Wellington but uses the very underrated fillet of pork. As a pig is considerably smaller than a cow, the circumference of the Wellington is smaller too, making a somewhat daintier dish. Try to avoid overlapping the pastry, if possible, or it can become a little stodgy; it should be crisp and well cooked.

→ 550G (1¼LB) PORK FILLET, WELL TRIMMED
→ 2 TBSP OLIVE OIL
→ 100G (4OZ) YOUNG LEAF SPINACH
→ 225G (8OZ) PUFF PASTRY
→ 50G (2OZ) SMOOTH LIVER PÂTÉ
→ 1 EGG, LIGHTLY BEATEN
→ SALT AND FRESHLY GROUND
   BLACK PEPPER
For the apple and sage compote:
→ 15G (½OZ) BUTTER
→ 2 SHALLOTS, FINELY CHOPPED
→ 2 CRISP APPLES (SUCH AS COX'S OR
   BRAEBURN), PEELED, CORED AND
   FINELY CHOPPED
→ 3–4 SAGE LEAVES, TORN
→ 100ML (3½FL OZ) DRY WHITE WINE
→ 100ML (3½FL OZ) VEGETABLE STOCK

1 Heat a heavy-based frying pan over a high heat. Season the pork fillet well and rub it all over with a little of the olive oil. Pour the remaining oil into the hot pan, add the pork fillet and sear until golden brown all over. Lower the heat a little and cook for 6–10 minutes, depending on the thickness of the fillet, turning often to cook evenly. Remove from the pan and leave to cool completely.

2 Next make the apple and sage compote. Heat the butter in the pan that the pork was cooked in, add the shallots and fry over a low heat until soft and translucent. Stir in the apples and sage leaves and cook for a couple of minutes, then add the wine and stock. Bring to the boil, reduce the heat and simmer for about 8 minutes. Purée the mixture, return to the pan and set aside.

3 Put 2 tablespoons of hot water into a pan and add the spinach. Cover and cook over a high heat for about 30 seconds, until the spinach wilts. Drain well, season to taste and leave to cool.

4 When the pork is cold, roll out the puff pastry so it is big enough to wrap around the fillet. Lay the cooled cooked spinach leaves in a line down the centre of the pastry. Spread the pâté over one side of the fillet, then place the fillet, pâté-side down, on the spinach.

5 Brush the edges of the pastry with the egg and wrap the pastry around the pork fillet, sealing the edges well and trimming away any excess pastry to create a neat parcel. Put the pork Wellington on a greased baking tray, seam-side down. Brush with the remaining egg and chill for 20 minutes. Preheat the oven to 200°C/400°F/Gas Mark 6.

6 Bake the Wellington for about 30 minutes, until the pastry is a rich, dark golden brown. Remove from the oven and leave to stand for 5 minutes before slicing. Reheat the apple and sage compote and serve with the pork Wellington.

Inspired by contestant Emma Corbett

Lamb Kofte with Fragrant Pilau Rice, Marinated Peppers and Tzatsiki

Some would call a variety of dishes on one plate a mezze, but in this case each one is essential to the success of the others. The kofte should be very well seasoned, as the rice can be a little sweet, so the meat and the tzatsiki are there to lift the dish.

→ 2 TSP CUMIN SEEDS
→ 2 TBSP CORIANDER SEEDS
→ 500G (1LB 2OZ) MINCED LAMB
→ JUICE OF 2 LEMONS
→ 4 TBSP CHOPPED MINT
→ 1 LARGE EGG, LIGHTLY BEATEN
→ 2 RED PEPPERS, HALVED AND DESEEDED
→ 2 GREEN PEPPERS, HALVED AND DESEEDED
→ 3 TBSP OLIVE OIL
→ SALT AND FRESHLY GROUND BLACK PEPPER

For the pilau rice:
→ 2 TBSP OLIVE OIL
→ 1 ONION, FINELY CHOPPED
→ 40G (1½OZ) PINE NUTS
→ 40G (1½OZ) CURRANTS
→ 1 CINNAMON STICK, HALVED
→ 1 GARLIC CLOVE, CRUSHED
→ 150G (5OZ) BASMATI RICE, RINSED WELL
→ 350ML (12FL OZ) VEGETABLE STOCK

For the tzatsiki:
→ 2 GARLIC CLOVES, PEELED
→ 150G (5OZ) PLAIN YOGHURT
→ 1 TBSP CHOPPED MINT

1 Preheat the oven to 220°C/425°F/Gas Mark 7.

2 Place the cumin and coriander seeds in a hot, dry frying pan and roast for 1–2 minutes. Crush in a pestle and mortar and set aside.

3 Put the lamb into a bowl and stir in half the lemon juice, plus the mint, crushed cumin and coriander. Season well. Bind with the egg and shape into 8 patties. Chill for 30 minutes.

4 Place the peppers on a baking tray and roast in the preheated oven for 20–30 minutes, until blackened and blistered. Put them in a bowl, cover with cling film and leave for 10 minutes, then peel off the skins. Slice the peppers thinly. Put them in a dish, toss with the remaining lemon juice and set aside.

5 For the rice, heat the olive oil in a large saucepan, add the onion and fry for 4–5 minutes, until golden. Stir in the pine nuts, currants, cinnamon and garlic and cook for 2 minutes, stirring constantly. Add the rice to the pan, stirring until well coated in the oil, and cook for 2 minutes. Add the stock and ½ teaspoon of salt. Stir once and cover with a tight-fitting lid, then reduce the heat to very low and cook for 15 minutes. All the liquid should have been absorbed and the rice should be fluffy and perfectly cooked.

6 To make the tzatsiki, put the garlic cloves into a pestle and mortar with a little salt and crush to a paste. Put the yoghurt into a small bowl and stir in the garlic and mint.

7 Next, cook the kofte. Heat the olive oil in a large frying pan, add the lamb patties and cook for about 5 minutes on each side, turning occasionally, until golden brown and cooked through.

8 Pile the rice on a large serving plate. Arrange the peppers in a line down the centre of the rice and top with the kofte, drizzled with a little tzatsiki. Serve the remaining tzatsiki separately.

Inspired by contestant Caroline Brewester

Moroccan Spiced Lamb

Lamb usually benefits from a good amount of fat when cooking, as it helps to keep the meat moist and to ensure that all the flavours are retained. However, in this recipe it is imperative that all the fat is removed or the subtle flavours of the spicing will be lost. Serve the lamb pink and succulent for best results.

→ 2 RACKS OF LAMB, WITH 6 CUTLETS EACH, TRIMMED OF ALL FAT
→ 200G (7OZ) WATERCRESS

For the marinade:
→ 4 GARLIC CLOVES, PEELED
→ 1 TSP SALT
→ 1 TSP GROUND CINNAMON
→ 1 TSP GROUND GINGER
→ 1 TSP GROUND ALLSPICE
→ 4 TBSP OLIVE OIL
→ 1 TBSP LEMON JUICE

For the salsa:
→ 3 VINE-RIPENED TOMATOES, SKINNED, DESEEDED AND DICED
→ ½ RED ONION, FINELY DICED
→ 1 TSP FINELY CHOPPED MILD RED CHILLI
→ 1 TBSP OLIVE OIL
→ 1 TBSP LEMON JUICE
→ 1 TBSP CHOPPED FRESH CORIANDER
→ SALT AND FRESHLY GROUND BLACK PEPPER

For the couscous:
→ A GOOD PINCH OF SAFFRON THREADS
→ 400ML (14FL OZ) VEGETABLE STOCK
→ 1 TBSP OLIVE OIL
→ 275G (10OZ) COUSCOUS
→ 20G (¾OZ) FLAT-LEAF PARSLEY, CHOPPED
→ 2 TBSP PINE NUTS, TOASTED
→ SEEDS FROM ½ POMEGRANATE

1 Preheat the oven to 200°C/400°F/Gas Mark 6. Bring the racks of lamb to room temperature.

2 For the marinade, crush the garlic to a paste with the salt in a pestle and mortar. Add the remaining marinade ingredients and mix well. Rub the mixture over the lamb and leave to marinate for about 20 minutes.

3 Meanwhile, for the salsa, mix the tomatoes, onion and chilli together in a bowl and stir in the olive oil, lemon juice, coriander and some salt and pepper. Set aside.

4 For the couscous, put the saffron threads in a large jug, add 1 tablespoon of hot water and leave to infuse for 10 minutes. Bring the stock to boiling point and add it to the saffron with the olive oil. Pour this mixture over the couscous. Cover with cling film and leave to stand for 5 minutes.

5 Separate the grains with a fork and stir in the parsley, pine nuts and pomegranate seeds.

6 Put the racks of lamb side by side in a roasting tin. Roast in the preheated oven for about 14 minutes (this will give pink meat). Remove from the oven, cover with foil and leave to rest for 5 minutes.

7 Place the couscous on a large plate and drizzle over a little of the salsa. Top with the racks of lamb and serve the remaining salsa separately. Accompany with a bowl of watercress.

Inspired by contestant Jacqueline Hillier

Spiced Lamb with Champ and Onions

Lamb and mash are a combination you can't resist! This is a simple dish with a few extras and bags of flavour. Traditional champ is mashed potato flavoured with spring onions. The whites are boiled in a little cream and the green tops are stirred in at the last minute. Here, parsnips and garlic make for an unusual twist on the classic.

→ 4 BONELESS LAMB LEG STEAKS, ABOUT 2.5CM (1 IN) THICK
→ 5 TBSP OLIVE OIL
→ 1 TSP BALSAMIC VINEGAR
→ JUICE OF ½ LEMON
→ 1 RED CHILLI, FINELY CHOPPED
→ 150ML (¼ PINT) HOT LAMB OR CHICKEN STOCK

For the champ:
→ 4 FLOURY POTATOES, SUCH AS MARIS PIPER, PEELED AND CHOPPED
→ 4 SMALL PARSNIPS, CHOPPED
→ 25G (1OZ) BUTTER
→ A BUNCH OF SPRING ONIONS, FINELY CHOPPED
→ 3 GARLIC CLOVES, FINELY CHOPPED
→ 2 TBSP CRÈME FRAÎCHE
→ 4 TBSP MILK

For the spiced onions:
→ 1 TBSP OLIVE OIL
→ 1 LARGE ONION, CHOPPED
→ 1 TSP GROUND CINNAMON
→ 4 DRIED DATES, CHOPPED
→ JUICE OF ½ LEMON
→ 1 TSP HARISSA PASTE
→ 2 TSP FINELY CHOPPED MINT
→ 2 TSP FINELY CHOPPED CORIANDER

1 Place the lamb steaks side by side in a non-metallic dish. In a small bowl, whisk 3 tablespoons of the olive oil with the balsamic vinegar, lemon juice and chilli. Pour this mixture over the lamb and leave to marinate in the fridge for at least 1 hour or overnight.

2 For the champ, cook the potatoes and parsnips in separate pans of boiling salted water until soft. Drain well and mash together until smooth. Cover and keep warm.

3 Heat the butter in a separate pan and fry the spring onions and garlic in it until soft. Stir into the mashed vegetables with the crème fraîche and milk. Mix together well, then cover and keep warm.

4 For the spiced onions, heat the oil in a frying pan, add the onion and cook gently until soft and translucent. Stir in the cinnamon, chopped dates, lemon juice and harissa and cook for 2 minutes over a medium heat. Remove from the heat and stir in the mint and coriander. Cover and keep warm.

5 Heat a heavy-based frying pan until very hot. Drain the marinade from the lamb steaks and reserve. Wipe the lamb dry on kitchen paper, then lightly brush it with the remaining olive oil. Sear the lamb steaks on both sides for 2 minutes. Reduce the heat a little and cook for a further 2 minutes per side for pink lamb. Remove from the pan, cover and keep warm.

6 Pour the reserved marinade into the frying pan, add the hot stock and bring to the boil, scraping up any sediment from the base of the pan.

7 Divide the champ between 4 warm serving plates. Top with the lamb steaks and spoon over the spiced onions. Drizzle with the pan juices and serve immediately.

Inspired by contestant Scott Ball

Lamb with Minted Lime Salsa and Chilli Roasted Vegetables

Many people associate eating lamb with Easter, but later-season lamb (say, late September) has a far superior flavour. The minted lime salsa gives the lamb the moisture it needs. The dish could also cope with a good blob of aïoli, or garlic mayonnaise (see page 118).

Remember to keep the lamb pink, as the more it is cooked, the drier it becomes (this doesn't apply, of course, if you are cooking it slowly in liquid – when making a stew, for example).

→ 2 SWEET POTATOES, PEELED AND CUT INTO CHUNKS
→ 4 SMALL MARIS PIPER POTATOES, PEELED AND HALVED
→ 2 PARSNIPS, CUT INTO CHUNKS
→ 1 RED ONION, SLICED INTO WEDGES
→ 1 GARLIC BULB, CUT HORIZONTALLY IN HALF
→ 5 TBSP OLIVE OIL
→ 1 MILD RED CHILLI, DESEEDED AND CHOPPED
→ 1 MILD GREEN CHILLI, DESEEDED AND CHOPPED
→ 8 LAMB LOIN CHOPS
→ SALT AND FRESHLY GROUND BLACK PEPPER

For the minted lime salsa:
→ 2 TBSP OLIVE OIL
→ 2 SHALLOTS, FINELY DICED
→ 2 TSP GRATED FRESH GINGER
→ 2 TBSP FINE-CUT LIME MARMALADE
→ JUICE AND GRATED ZEST OF 1 LIME
→ 2 TBSP CHOPPED MINT
→ 1 TBSP CHOPPED CORIANDER

1 Preheat the oven to 220°C/425°F/Gas Mark 7.

2 Put the potatoes, parsnips, red onion and garlic in a shallow baking dish. Drizzle 3 tablespoons of the olive oil over the vegetables and season with salt and pepper. Place in the oven and roast for 30 minutes. Stir in the chillies 5 minutes before the end of cooking.

3 For the salsa, mix all the ingredients together and set aside.

4 Heat the remaining olive oil in a heavy-based frying pan. Season the lamb chops, add to the pan and sear for 5–6 minutes on each side (you will need to cook them in batches). Cover and keep warm.

5 Arrange the roasted vegetables and lamb chops in a serving dish. Spoon the minted lime salsa over the chops and serve.

Inspired by contestant Karen Gemmel

Minted Lamb and Rosemary Kebabs with Roasted Vegetables

Lamb and rosemary, what can you say? What a classic, and then served with mint sauce – wow! An underrated cut of meat, lamb neck fillets are tender and full of flavour. Ask your butcher to remove most of the fat, or slip a sharp knife under the fat and gently slide the blade from one end to the other. The meat is delicate and will cook very quickly, so prepare all the rest of the ingredients before cooking the kebabs.

→ 5 SMALL, FLOURY POTATOES, SUCH AS MARIS PIPER, PEELED AND CUT INTO GOOD-SIZED CHUNKS
→ 1 RED PEPPER, HALVED AND DESEEDED
→ 1 GREEN PEPPER, HALVED AND DESEEDED
→ 1 RED ONION, ROUGHLY CHOPPED
→ 100ML (3½FL OZ) OLIVE OIL
→ 100G (4OZ) GREEN BEANS
→ 2 X 350G (12OZ) LAMB NECK FILLETS, CUT INTO 2CM (¾ IN) DICE
→ 8 LONG, WOODY ROSEMARY SPRIGS TO USE AS SKEWERS (OR 8 BAMBOO SKEWERS AND A FEW SPRIGS OF ROSEMARY)
→ 200ML (7FL OZ) RED WINE
→ 2 TSP MINT JELLY
→ SALT AND FRESHLY GROUND BLACK PEPPER

1 Preheat the oven to 220°C/425°F/Gas Mark 7.

2 Put the potatoes, peppers and onion in a roasting tin, pour in half the oil and toss to coat. Place in the oven and roast for 20 minutes.

3 Remove the vegetables from the oven. Put the peppers in a bowl and cover them with cling film for 10 minutes to loosen the skin. Skin the peppers and roughly chop them into chunks. Put to one side with the onion, cover and keep warm. Return the potatoes to the oven.

4 Blanch the green beans in boiling salted water for 1 minute, then drain, refresh in cold water and drain again. Set aside.

5 Skewer the lamb on to the 8 rosemary 'sticks' (or on to 8 bamboo skewers, placing the sprigs of rosemary between the meat) and season well. Heat the remaining oil in a large frying pan. Sear the skewered lamb for 4 minutes on each side, then transfer to the oven, placing it on top of the potatoes. Cook for 5 minutes.

6 Meanwhile, pour the red wine into the frying pan and cook over a high heat, scraping up any sediment from the base of the pan with a wooden spoon. Boil until the wine is reduced by half, then stir in the mint jelly. Transfer to a serving jug and keep warm.

7 Remove the roasting tin from the oven. Transfer the lamb kebabs to a plate and keep warm. Drain away any excess oil from the tin and stir in the peppers, onion and blanched green beans. Heat through for a couple of minutes in the oven.

8 Arrange the lamb kebabs on top of the roasted vegetables. Serve with the minted red wine sauce.

Masterchef Masterclass
John Torode's Roast Poultry

Roasting a bird or a joint of meat on a Sunday is a memory from a bygone era for many of us. Our lifestyles have changed so much that it is the sound of cash registers we hear now, rather than the sizzle of roasted meat. It is no longer the norm for the smell of crisp, well-seasoned meat, and potatoes, carrots and parsnips caramelising in the oven, to be wafting through the house as friends and family arrive for Sunday lunch. Maybe I can persuade you not to go shopping but to turn on the oven instead and get roasting.

A roast should be a treat, but you are not going to get the true taste of roast chicken (or duck, or turkey or any other fowl) unless you buy a decent bird. Never forget that if the bird has lived well, you will eat well. Freedom to roam and a diet based on grain are essential to the flavour, which means you need to buy at least a free-range bird, preferably an organic one. Free-range birds vary considerably in quality, from ones that have been kept in conditions that barely improve upon standard broiler houses to ones that have had the full run of the farmyard and been fed on maize. Organic birds are reared and fed according to strictly monitored welfare standards.

Once you've selected your bird, cooking it is comparatively simple, but there are a few general rules to observe:

→ Choose a roasting tin that is the correct size for your bird. There should be enough space around the bird for the juices to flow but not so much space that they will spread thinly and burn.

→ Most birds need some fat added before cooking, to keep them moist and help crisp up the skin. You can rub oil or butter over them, or lay strips of bacon over the top.

→ Season the bird well inside and out.

→ Make sure the oven is preheated to the correct temperature before putting the bird in.

→ Calculate an approximate cooking time before you put the bird in the oven. In general, a chicken will take 1–1¼ hours, a duck about 1½ hours and a turkey can take as long as 3 hours, depending on size.

→ To test whether the bird is done, insert a knife between the thigh and the breast; if the juices run clear rather than pink, it is ready.

→ Leave the bird to rest in a warm place for 10–15 minutes before serving. This results in tender, succulent meat.

John Torode's Roast Duck with Caramelised Onions

SERVES 4

→ 1 X 2.8KG (6LB) DUCK
→ A FEW SPRIGS OF THYME
→ A FEW SPRIGS OF ROSEMARY
→ 1 WHOLE BULB OF GARLIC
→ 2 ONIONS
→ 6 SMOKED STREAKY BACON
 RASHERS
→ 1 TSP PLAIN FLOUR
→ SALT AND FRESHLY
 GROUND BLACK PEPPER

A roast is easy to prepare in advance and then all you need to do is put it in the oven. Duck is one of the great roasting birds but many people dislike it – usually because they have been served it either dry and overcooked or fatty and tough. The majority of the time, I'm sorry to say, this is the cook's fault. A well-roasted duck is a thing of joy: sweet, deep in flavour, not overpowering, with soft meat under wonderfully crisp skin. Wild ducks can be stringy if they are old but young ducks should be moist and delicious. Admittedly the meat yield is lower than that of a chicken but the flavour is far superior.

I like to use Barbary duck and to cook it well done, so it is almost falling off the bone. Any leftover meat can be used in a salad the next day. A simple spinach, duck and poached egg salad with a little goat's cheese is a nice treat.

1 Using kitchen paper, wipe the duck clean inside and out and remove the excess fat. Season the duck inside and out and put the thyme, rosemary, whole garlic bulb and 120ml (4fl oz) of water in the cavity. Leave in the fridge until 2 hours before roasting (I prefer to do it the day before), then bring to room temperature.

2 Preheat the oven to 220°C/425°F/Gas Mark 7. Place the duck on a rack in a roasting tin and pour 400ml (14fl oz) water into the tin. Cut the onions in half, leaving the skin on, and place them around the bird. Lay the bacon over the breast, cover the tin with aluminium foil and seal the edges. Place in the oven and roast for 30 minutes.

3 Take the duck out of the oven and reduce the heat to 200°C/ 400°F/Gas Mark 6. Remove the foil and bacon (the bacon is delicious on buttered fresh white bread), then return the duck to the oven and cook for 1 hour, basting twice.

4 Remove the bird from the oven and check that it is done (see page 95). Leave to rest in a warm place while you make the gravy.

5 Drain the cooking liquid from the roasting tin into a jug and set aside. Return the dry roasting tin to the hob, add the onions, cut-side down, and cook for a few minutes, until they colour slightly. Sprinkle in the flour and stir for a few minutes.

6 By now the cooking liquid should have separated – skim off the fat and discard, then pour the cooking liquid into the roasting tin. Open the cavity of the duck slightly, drain off the juices and add to the roasting tin. Bring to the boil, stirring constantly, and simmer until reduced to a gravy. Taste and adjust the seasoning.

7 Return the duck to the oven for 15 minutes to crisp up, then serve with the gravy.

Roast Duck with Red Wine and Sour Cherry Sauce and Sweet Potato Mash

Well, you really can't go wrong with this combination. It's a real crowd-pleaser for both Easter and Christmas. You may find it easier to serve it in the middle of the table and let everyone help themselves rather than as a plate of food, as it can look a little messy.

- → 2–2.25KG (4½–5LB) GRESSINGHAM DUCK
- → 150G (5OZ) DRIED SOUR CHERRIES
- → 300ML (½ PINT) DRY RED WINE
- → 50G (2OZ) GRANULATED SUGAR
- → 2 TBSP GOOD-QUALITY RED WINE VINEGAR
- → SEA SALT AND FRESHLY GROUND BLACK PEPPER

For the sweet potato mash:
- → 2 SWEET POTATOES
- → 1 SMALL SWEDE, CUT INTO CHUNKS
- → A GOOD KNOB OF BUTTER
- → 2 TBSP SINGLE CREAM

For the cabbage:
- → 1 SAVOY CABBAGE, CORED AND FINELY SHREDDED
- → 150G (5OZ) SMOKED STREAKY BACON, CUT INTO FINE STRIPS
- → 15G (½OZ) BUTTER

1 Preheat the oven to 220°C/425°F/Gas Mark 7.

2 Trim and discard any loose fat from the duck cavity. Prick the duck all over with a sharp knife and sprinkle with sea salt, rubbing it into the skin. Season with black pepper. Place the duck on a rack in a roasting tin and roast for 20 minutes. Reduce the oven temperature to 200°C/400°F/Gas Mark 6 and cook the duck for about an hour longer, depending on size.

3 For the sauce, place the cherries, red wine, sugar and red wine vinegar in a pan and bring to a simmer. Reduce the heat to barely simmering and cook, uncovered, for 50 minutes–1 hour, stirring occasionally, until the sauce has reduced and thickened.

4 When the duck has about 45 minutes left to cook, prepare the mash. Put the unpeeled sweet potatoes on a tray in the oven with the duck and roast for 45 minutes, until tender. Cook the swede in boiling salted water until tender, then drain and return to the pan. Scoop out the soft flesh from the sweet potatoes, discarding the skin. Mash the swede and sweet potato together with the butter and cream. Heat through gently for a couple of minutes, then season with salt and plenty of black pepper. Keep warm.

5 To test if the duck is done, push a skewer into the thickest part of the flesh; if the juices run clear, it is ready. Remove from the oven, turn upside down and cover loosely with foil. Leave to rest.

6 Cook the shredded cabbage in a large pan of boiling salted water for 2–3 minutes, then drain and refresh in cold water. In a large frying pan, cook the bacon in the butter for 2–3 minutes. Stir in the cabbage, then cover and cook for 3 minutes, until the cabbage is tender but still has a little bite. Adjust the seasoning.

7 Transfer the duck to a serving platter and serve with the sour cherry sauce, sweet potato mash and cabbage.

Inspired by contestant Sarah Thomas

Seared Duck Breast with Chilli Greens

Try to find a Barbary duck for this recipe – it's bigger and of superior quality. The slow cooking at the start of this recipe, where the fat is rendered from under the skin, is important: this fat is then used to baste the meat and keep it as moist as possible.

→ 4 DUCK BREASTS
→ LEAVES FROM 4 SPRIGS OF THYME
→ 2 TBSP RUNNY HONEY
→ 2 TBSP SOY SAUCE
→ 4 TBSP ORANGE JUICE
→ 4 TBSP WHITE WINE VINEGAR
→ 1 TSP CASTER SUGAR
→ 25G (1OZ) CLARIFIED BUTTER
→ SALT AND FRESHLY GROUND
   BLACK PEPPER
   For the chilli greens:
→ 150G (5OZ) BROCCOLI
→ 100G (4OZ) FRENCH BEANS, TRIMMED
→ 1 PAK CHOY, CUT INTO QUARTERS
→ 1 TBSP GROUNDNUT OIL
→ 1 MILD LONG RED CHILLI, FINELY CHOPPED
→ 1 GARLIC CLOVE, FINELY CHOPPED

1 Preheat the oven to 200°C/400°F/Gas Mark 6.

2 Score the skin of the duck with a sharp knife. Put the duck breasts in a shallow dish and season with salt and pepper. Rub the thyme leaves, honey and soy sauce into the scored duck skin and leave to marinate for 10 minutes.

3 Mix the orange juice, vinegar and sugar together in a small jug and set aside.

4 Heat a large, heavy-based ovenproof frying pan over a medium heat and melt the butter in it. Place the duck breasts in the pan, skin-side down, and cook slowly for about 5 minutes, so the fat renders from under the skin and the skin becomes golden brown.

5 Turn the duck over and transfer the pan to the oven. Cook for 5–7 minutes, until the duck is cooked but still pink in the centre. Transfer the duck to a plate, cover and keep warm.

6 Strain off about half the fat from the frying pan. Add the orange juice mixture to the pan, together with any marinade, and place on the hob over a fairly high heat. Simmer until reduced by about half to a fairly thick syrup. Remove from the heat and keep warm.

7 Steam the vegetables over boiling water for about 3 minutes; they should remain slightly crisp. Meanwhile, heat the groundnut oil in a frying pan, add the chilli and garlic and fry for about 30 seconds, just to release their flavour. Add the steamed vegetables and stir-fry for 2–3 minutes in the chilli and garlic oil. Season to taste and remove from the heat.

8 Slice the duck breasts and pour any meat juices into the sauce. Reheat the sauce gently. Arrange the chilli greens and slices of duck on a plate and drizzle with a little of the sauce. Pour the remainder into a jug and serve immediately.

Masterchef Masterclass
John Torode's Burger

Burgers are so ubiquitous that you may wonder what is the point of making them at home. Well, the point is that they will be a lot better than most of the ones you can buy. And, of course, it means you can make them exactly to your liking.

The perfect burger should be big and juicy, even when cooked well done. To achieve this, you need to include fat in the mince. I like to use 40 per cent fat, which I know sounds a lot but it effectively bastes the meat during cooking, ensuring it stays moist. Most of it will drain off, leaving you with a succulent, well-flavoured but not overly fatty burger.

The meat for burgers should be coarsely minced. Most butchers mince their meat on a medium setting, so you may have to ask to have yours done separately. Or you can mince it yourself at home if you have a mincer. Chuck, skirt and rump are all good choices but remember to ask the butcher to include some fat.

I have another little secret when it comes to burgers. Instead of salt I use oyster sauce to season the meat. I find salt can make the mixture dry and crumbly because it draws out water, whereas if you use oyster sauce the meat stays moist and binds together well.

To get the best results, follow the tips below:
→ Use meat straight from the fridge and make sure it is well chilled. This will help it to bind together.
→ Mix everything together as quickly and lightly as possible, preferably with your hands.
→ Dampen your hands slightly before shaping the burgers, so that the mixture doesn't stick to them.
→ Cook the burgers in a very hot, heavy-based pan and resist the temptation to move them about before they have formed a good crust underneath – otherwise they will stick.
→ If you cook your burgers on a barbecue, light the fire well in advance and make sure it has died down to glowing, reddish-grey coals before you start cooking.

John Torode's
Basic Beefburger

SERVES 6 LARGE BURGERS
→ 1.5KG (3¼LB) MINCED BEEF,
   IDEALLY CONTAINING
   40 PER CENT FAT
→ 2 RED ONIONS, FINELY DICED
→ A GOOD HANDFUL OF FLAT-LEAF
   PARSLEY, FINELY CHOPPED
→ 3 TBSP TOMATO KETCHUP
→ 3 TBSP OYSTER SAUCE
→ 1 EGG YOLK
   To serve:
→ 6 LARGE, SOFT WHITE BUNS,
   LIGHTLY TOASTED
→ LETTUCE, TOMATO, GHERKINS,
   ONION, AVOCADO, KETCHUP,
   MAYONNAISE – WHATEVER
   TAKES YOUR FANCY

1 Put all the ingredients in a large bowl. With your hands or a large spoon, mix everything together until it is evenly combined.

2 Divide the mixture into 6 portions and roll each one into a large ball. Flatten slightly with the palm of your hand, then place them in the fridge. If possible, chill for a good hour.

3 To cook the burgers, either have a barbecue good and hot, with the coals glowing, or heat a ridged griddle pan or heavy-based frying pan. Do not add any oil. Place the burgers on the barbecue rack or in the pan and leave for a few minutes, until the edges start to colour.

4 Slide a metal spatula under each burger and flip it over. Cook for a few minutes, then turn again. If using a frying pan or griddle pan, reduce the heat; on a barbecue just move the burgers to the sides, which should be slightly cooler. Leave the burgers to cook for anything from 8–15 minutes, depending on how well done you like them.

5 Serve in lightly toasted buns, with the accompaniments of your choice.

Inspired by contestant James Millen

Sirloin Steak with Black Pepper Crust and Rösti Potatoes

A great steak is something to be revered. Quality is paramount, so you should visit a good butcher's when shopping for this recipe. Treat the steak with the respect it deserves. To prevent it being overpowered by the pepper, sift the crushed peppercorns in a fine sieve to remove any dust before using. A generous garnish of watercress is needed to freshen up the dish.

- → 2 PARSNIPS, CHOPPED
- → 1 TBSP HORSERADISH SAUCE
- → 4 TABLESPOONS SINGLE CREAM
- → 50G (2OZ) BUTTER
- → 4 X 200G (7OZ) THICK SIRLOIN STEAKS
- → OIL FOR BRUSHING
- → 4 TBSP COARSELY CRUSHED BLACK PEPPERCORNS
- → 1 RAW BEETROOT, PARBOILED
- → 75G (3OZ) WATERCRESS
- → A FEW DROPS OF BALSAMIC VINEGAR
- → SALT AND FRESHLY GROUND BLACK PEPPER

For the rösti:
- → 550G (1¼LB) POTATOES, PREFERABLY KING EDWARD, PEELED AND GRATED
- → 1 ONION, FINELY CHOPPED
- → 25G (1OZ) LARDONS, FINELY CHOPPED
- → 1 EGG, BEATEN
- → 1 TBSP CHOPPED SAGE
- → 2 TSP GRAINY MUSTARD
- → 4 TBSP OLIVE OIL

MASTERCHEF TOP TIP
I know most people are concerned about the amount of fat they eat, and rightly so. But beef needs fat for flavour, so you must cook steak with a decent amount of fat still on. Just remember that you don't have to eat the fat; you can cut it off after cooking, if you want. Or put it to one side and I'll eat it!
Gregg Wallace, Masterchef Judge

1 For the rösti, put the grated potato in a sieve over a bowl. Season with plenty of salt to extract the juice and set aside for 20 minutes. Squeeze the potato dry between layers of kitchen paper.

2 Put the potato in a bowl with the onion, lardons, egg, sage and mustard and mix well. Shape the mixture into 8 flat cakes, either by hand or by pressing it into 7cm (2¾ in) metal rings.

3 Heat the olive oil in a large frying pan, add the rösti and fry until golden brown on each side. Drain on kitchen paper and keep warm.

4 Cook the parsnips in boiling salted water until tender, then drain well. Mash to a soft purée with the horseradish, cream and half the butter. Season to taste, then cover and keep warm.

5 Preheat a heavy-based frying pan or ridged griddle. Brush the steaks with oil and season with salt, then roll them in the black pepper.

6 Put the steaks in the pan and brown them quickly on both sides over a high heat, then reduce the heat and cook gently for the remaining time – about 4 minutes per side for a medium-rare steak. Leave to rest in a warm place.

7 Meanwhile, peel the beetroot and slice it thickly. Heat the remaining butter in a frying pan, add the beetroot slices and cook over a medium heat until crisp on the outside but tender inside.

8 Arrange the steaks, rösti, creamed parsnip and fried beetroot on serving plates. Garnish with the watercress and a few drops of balsamic vinegar. Serve immediately.

Masterchef Masterclass
John Torode's Steak

Cooking steak is deceptively simple. In theory, there's nothing more to it than slapping a steak in a hot pan. In practice, there are so many variables that you need to devote a little more care and attention to it than this might imply.

First, shop wisely for your steak. Visit a good butcher who will cut the steak to your liking and should be able to tell you something about the quality of the meat and where it came from. Alternatively, go direct to a producer – increasingly easy these days, with the spread of farmers' markets and Internet shopping (see List of Suppliers, pages 188–90).

Many people choose steak by looking for something that is uniformly red and not at all fatty, whereas a good steak needs some marbling – tiny veins of fat that melt into the meat and keep it moist during cooking. I prefer not to buy steak surrounded by yellow fat, as that usually means it comes from a herd that has been fed on grain rather than grass. Grass-fed herds, which will have been allowed to roam free, produce meat with milky-white fat that has the lovely, earthy flavour I prefer.

Fillet is usually thought of as the best cut, and because you get only two very small fillets from each beast, the laws of supply and demand dictate that it is extremely expensive. Sirloin is usually seen as next best, with rump coming a poor third. Ever game for a bit of controversy, I disagree with this. I really love a thick piece of rump cut from a piece of beef that has been hung on the bone for twenty-one days to mature. Pan-fry it very quickly in a really hot pan, then finish it off in the oven for 5–10 minutes until it is medium rare – fantastic stuff! A really classy piece of rump has all the right ratios of fat, muscle structure, fibre and flavour.

Everyone has their own opinion about how they like their steak done. If you follow the guidelines below, you should end up with your personal idea of steak heaven.

- Use a heavy-based frying pan or a cast-iron griddle to cook the steak. These retain the heat well and ensure it is evenly distributed.
- Brush the steak, rather than the pan, with oil and season it with salt and pepper just before cooking. Then get the pan almost smoking hot, lay the steak in it and sear it over a very high heat without disturbing it. When it has browned and slightly caramelised underneath, turn and cook the other side.
- For large, medium-rare steaks allow about 3 minutes per side. Increase or decrease this by about a minute per side if you prefer medium or rare steak respectively.
- Alternatively, you can sear the steak briefly on each side, then transfer it to a hot oven (about 200°C/400°F/Gas Mark 6) for 5–8 minutes, depending on how well done you like it.
- Let the steak rest on a warm plate for a few minutes before serving. This allows the tissues to relax and become more tender.
- Finally, since cooking times can only ever be approximate, it is worth knowing a chef's trick for testing whether steak is done to your liking. It works better for a firmer steak such as sirloin or rump rather than fillet, as fillet tends to be very spongy. While the steak is cooking, touch it with your finger. Then, using your right hand place the tip of your thumb on the tip of your little finger. Now touch the cushion of fat at the base of your thumb with your left hand – the resistance given by the thumb in this position is the same as a well-done steak. Open your right hand completely and relax it, then touch the cushion beneath your thumb again – the resistance felt now is the same as rare steak. Halfway between will be medium.

John Torode's
Steak Béarnaise

SERVES 4
- → 4 RUMP OR SIRLOIN STEAKS, WEIGHING ABOUT 300G (11OZ) EACH
- → A LITTLE OLIVE OIL
- → SALT AND FRESHLY GROUND BLACK PEPPER
- → A BUNCH OF WATERCRESS, TO SERVE

For the béarnaise sauce:
- → A FEW SPRIGS OF TARRAGON
- → 100ML (3¹/₂FL OZ) WHITE WINE VINEGAR
- → 1 SHALLOT, CHOPPED
- → 2 EGG YOLKS
- → 120G (4¹/₂OZ) WARM MELTED BUTTER

MASTERCHEF TOP TIP
As with mustard or horseradish sauce, béarnaise should be served in small quantities alongside the meat or fish but never over it.

Steak with béarnaise sauce is a classic dish that will never go out of fashion – especially when served with a bowl of crisp, freshly cooked chips (see page 66). Béarnaise is similar to hollandaise (see pages 20–1) but even richer, and flavoured with tarragon. Used as an accompaniment to meat and fish, it is always served at room temperature and should have a good kick to it from the initial vinegar reduction.

1 To make the sauce, strip the tarragon leaves from their stalks, chop them and set aside. Crush the stalks between your fingers to release the oils.

2 Put the vinegar, shallot and tarragon stalks in a small saucepan and bring to the boil. Simmer until reduced by about three-quarters, then leave to cool.

3 Strain the vinegar reduction into a heatproof glass bowl. Place the bowl over a pan of barely simmering water, making sure the water does not touch the base of the bowl.

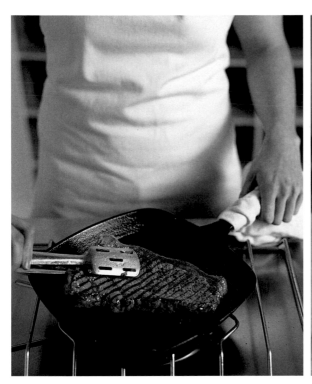

Add the egg yolks and whisk for 2–3 minutes, until the mixture turns pale and thick and the whisk leaves a trail on the surface when lifted.

4 Remove the bowl from the heat and put it on a folded cloth on a work surface. Start to whisk in the melted butter, little by little, making sure that each addition has been thoroughly incorporated before the next. Continue whisking in this way until all the butter has been used or your arm has fallen off! If the sauce gets too thick at any stage, add a few drops of hot water from the saucepan.

5 Season the sauce with salt and pepper and stir in the chopped tarragon. The sauce should taste sharp and well seasoned. Remember that it is for flavouring the meat and should have a good punch to it.

6 Preheat a heavy frying pan or a ridged griddle until almost smoking hot. Season the steaks with lots of salt and pepper and rub well with olive oil, then cook as described on page 107. Rest briefly in a warm place, then serve with the watercress and béarnaise sauce on the side.

Venison Fillet with Raspberry Sauce and Braised Chicory

This combination of well-seared venison, a sharp sauce and the soft and slightly bitter chicory makes for a very good plate of food indeed. Served as a starter with some sheep's milk cheese, braised chicory would make a real treat.

→ 4 X 150G (5OZ) VENISON FILLET STEAKS
→ 150ML (¼ PINT) OLIVE OIL
→ 4 TBSP ROBUST RED WINE
→ 3 TBSP CHOPPED MINT
→ 3 TBSP CHOPPED SAGE
→ 3 TBSP CHOPPED MARJORAM
→ 225G (8OZ) RASPBERRIES
→ 300ML (½ PINT) BEEF STOCK
→ 2 TBSP FRAMBOISE LIQUEUR OR BRANDY
→ 10G (⅓OZ) GOOD-QUALITY PLAIN CHOCOLATE (AT LEAST 70 PER CENT COCOA SOLIDS), GRATED
→ SALT AND FRESHLY GROUND BLACK PEPPER

For the braised chicory:
→ 3 TBSP LEMON JUICE
→ 2 TBSP CASTER SUGAR
→ 4 HEADS OF CHICORY, TRIMMED
→ 40G (1½OZ) BUTTER

Ⓜ MASTERCHEF TOP TIP

When buying venison, look for deep red meat with clear, bright fat. Strangely, this fat is not good to eat, so remove it before cooking. If, like me, you enjoy a gamy flavour from your dead Bambi, ask your butcher if the meat has been hung. Anywhere between 12 and 21 days is good.
Gregg Wallace, Masterchef Judge

1 Put the venison in a shallow dish in a single layer. Mix 120ml (4fl oz) of the olive oil with the red wine and herbs. Lightly crush the raspberries, reserving a few for garnish, and stir them into the oil and herb mixture. Pour this mixture over the venison steaks, then cover and leave in the fridge to marinate for 24 hours.

2 Remove the meat from the marinade, dry it well and put to one side to come to room temperature.

3 Meanwhile, liquidise the marinade and strain through a sieve into a saucepan. Season with a little salt and pepper, then stir in the beef stock. Bring to the boil and cook over a high heat until reduced by half. Add the framboise or brandy and boil vigorously for 2 minutes. Skim off any surface oil. Whisk the chocolate into the sauce, adjust the seasoning if necessary and keep warm.

4 For the chicory, bring a saucepan of water to the boil and add the lemon juice, half the sugar and the chicory. Cover and cook for 30 minutes, until the chicory is soft. Drain and arrange the chicory in a dish in a single layer. Sprinkle with ½ tablespoon of the remaining sugar and some salt and pepper and leave to cool.

5 Gently squeeze each chicory head in kitchen paper to extract the bitter juices. Melt the butter in a large frying pan over a medium heat. Add the chicory in a single layer and brown evenly all over. Remove from the pan and drain well, then transfer to a warm serving dish. Sprinkle with the remaining caster sugar and adjust the seasoning.

6 Heat the remaining olive oil in a large frying pan, add the venison steaks and fry over a high heat for about 4 minutes on each side.

7 Transfer the steaks to warm plates, pour over the sauce and garnish with the reserved raspberries. Serve with the chicory.

Inspired by contestant Caroline Brewester

Venison Fillet with Celeriac Mash and Damson Sauce

Caroline found herself an excellent farmers' market and good damsons when shopping for this dish. Damsons are cooking plums with a rich purple colour and a slightly sharp flavour. This is important as it gives the sauce body and structure. Use a generous amount of pepper, as the venison likes it and they sit very well together.

→ 1 TSP JUNIPER BERRIES, CRUSHED

→ 150ML (¼ PINT) GOOD-QUALITY
BEEF STOCK

→ 4 X 150G (5OZ) VENISON FILLET STEAKS,
ABOUT 2.5CM (1 IN) THICK

→ 1 TBSP OLIVE OIL

→ 25G (1OZ) BUTTER, CHILLED

→ 1 GLASS OF RED WINE

→ 1 TBSP DAMSON JELLY

→ SALT AND FRESHLY GROUND
BLACK PEPPER

For the celeriac mash:

→ 3 FLOURY POTATOES, SUCH AS MARIS
PIPER, PEELED AND CHOPPED

→ 1 CELERIAC, PEELED AND DICED

→ ABOUT 300ML (½ PINT) MILK

→ 4 TBSP SINGLE CREAM

→ 25G (1OZ) BUTTER

→ ½ TSP FRESHLY GRATED NUTMEG

1 Place the juniper berries in a small saucepan with the stock and bring to the boil. Reduce the heat and simmer for 2 minutes, then remove from the heat and leave to infuse for 30 minutes. Strain and set aside.

2 For the celeriac mash, cook the potatoes in a pan of boiling salted water until tender. Put the celeriac in a small pan and add enough milk just to cover, then bring to the boil and cook until tender.

3 Drain the potatoes well and mash. Drain the celeriac, reserving the milk, and mash. Beat the 2 vegetables together with the cream, butter and enough of the reserved milk to make a smooth, thick purée. Stir in the nutmeg and season with salt and pepper to taste. Cover and keep warm.

4 Pat the venison steaks dry on kitchen paper and season well. Heat a heavy-based frying pan until very hot, then add the oil and half the butter. Add the venison and cook for about 4 minutes on each side. Transfer the venison to a plate, cover and keep warm.

5 Pour the red wine and stock into the frying pan and boil until reduced by half, stirring up any sediment from the base of the pan. Stir in the damson jelly and any meat juices from the plate of venison. Whisk the remaining butter into the sauce and check the seasoning.

6 Place the celeriac mash on 4 warmed plates with the venison steaks. Spoon the sauce over the venison and serve immediately.

Salads and Vegetarian

Masterchef Masterclass
John Torode's Vinaigrette and Mayonnaise

Salad dressings such as mayonnaise and vinaigrette can enhance the humble lettuce leaf and bring a new dimension to even the simplest salads. Mayonnaise is one of the most versatile sauces ever invented, yet it is based on just two ingredients: eggs and oil. To that base you can add a variety of flavourings: lemon, mustard or garlic; blanched green vegetables such as spinach and watercress; herbs such as basil, parsley, dill, tarragon and chives; or piquant ingredients such as capers, horseradish, anchovies and finely chopped gherkins. Flavoured mayonnaise can be served not just with salads but with fish, poultry, meat and vegetables.

Like hollandaise (see pages 20–1), mayonnaise is an emulsified sauce. The secret of success is to beat the oil into the yolks very slowly – just a drop at a time initially – until the mixture thickens.

Vinaigrette is a simple oil and vinegar emulsion, which, unlike mayonnaise, is not expected to remain stable. It couldn't be easier to make but the crucial thing is to get the balance of flavours right. It should be tart but rounded, viscous but not oily, and full-flavoured but not overpowering. Its character varies depending on the type of oil used, the type of vinegar (or you can substitute lemon juice), and whether it includes mustard, herbs and other flavourings.

Here are some tips for success when making mayonnaise:

→ Make sure all the ingredients are at room temperature before you start, then the mixture is less likely to separate.

→ Rather than olive oil, I prefer to use vegetable oil. Olive oil is too strong and can leave an unpleasant aftertaste. If you use a generous amount of vinegar and mustard, they provide all the flavour you need.

→ Place the bowl on a cloth before you start whisking, to stop it moving around.

→ Add the oil to the other ingredients a drop at a time to begin with, whisking like crazy (it helps to have someone else adding the oil while you whisk). Then after you have added about a third of the oil and the emulsion has been established, you can pour in the rest in a thin, steady stream.

→ If the mayonnaise looks as if it is starting to curdle, you may be able to bring it back together by whisking in a few drops of hot water. If the worst happens and it separates, you can usually save it by starting again with another egg yolk in a clean bowl and whisking the separated mixture into it a drop at a time.

→ If the finished mayonnaise is too thick, whisk in a little hot water or lemon juice.

→ I always use white pepper rather than black for seasoning mayonnaise, so that the specks don't make the sauce look dirty.

John Torode's
Vinaigrette

MAKES ABOUT 400ML (14FL OZ)
→ 1 TBSP DIJON MUSTARD
→ 5 TBSP RED WINE VINEGAR
→ 1 TSP WALNUT OIL
→ 300ML (½ PINT) EXTRA
  VIRGIN OLIVE OIL
→ SEA SALT AND FRESHLY
  GROUND BLACK PEPPER

This is my favourite dressing, which I learned to make when I first started working in a commercial kitchen. It's good with crisp salad leaves such as Cos or iceberg, and also with asparagus or cooled, slightly underdone green beans.

When you are buying salad leaves, look for decent-sized heads that are as fresh as possible, without browned or wilting edges. The outer layer should be discarded (give it to your pet rabbit, if you have one), as it will have been exposed to the air and therefore not as crisp as the inner leaves.

Wash salad leaves gently in cool water. The way I do this is to fill the sink with water and drop the leaves on top. Then I gently push them under the water and turn them over to clean them. The dirt should sink to the bottom while the leaves float and escape bruising. Lift the leaves gently from the water a handful at a time, and either shake them dry or use a salad spinner.

Never drown your salad leaves in dressing: you should toss them in just enough dressing to coat. Too much will make the leaves limp and unpleasant in texture.

1 Place the mustard and vinegar in a bowl and whisk until blended.

2 Gradually whisk in the walnut and olive oils in a thin, steady stream, then season with salt and pepper. Taste and adjust the seasoning with more mustard, vinegar, oil, salt or pepper as necessary.

3 The vinaigrette will keep in an airtight jar in the fridge for up to 1 month. Bring to room temperature before using and whisk briefly (or shake the jar) to combine the ingredients.

John Torode's
Mayonnaise

MAKES ABOUT 300ML (½ PINT)
→ 3 EGG YOLKS
→ 1 TBSP DIJON MUSTARD
→ 1 TBSP WHITE WINE VINEGAR
→ 250ML (8FL OZ) VEGETABLE OIL
→ A SQUEEZE OF LEMON JUICE
→ SALT AND WHITE PEPPER

1 Put the egg yolks in a small bowl with the mustard and vinegar. Whisk together until smooth and almost white.

2 Add the oil a drop at a time, whisking constantly. After adding about a third of the oil, the mixture should have thickened considerably. Add a few drops of hot water if it is too thick to whisk.

3 Pour in the rest of the oil in a thin, steady stream, still whisking, until you have a smooth, glossy mayonnaise that is thick enough to stand in peaks.

4 Adjust the seasoning with lemon juice, salt and pepper, plus more vinegar if necessary. The mayonnaise will keep in the fridge for 4 days.

John Torode's
Aïoli

MAKES 350ML (12FL OZ)
→ 1 LARGE GARLIC CLOVE
→ 2 EGG YOLKS
→ 300ML (½ PINT) LIGHT OLIVE OIL
   (OR EQUAL PARTS EXTRA VIRGIN
   OLIVE OIL AND SUNFLOWER OIL)
→ JUICE OF ½ LEMON
→ SALT AND WHITE PEPPER

Aïoli is a garlic-flavoured mayonnaise originating from the South of France. It adds a real kick to hot dishes such as grilled fish and roast lamb, and also goes well with a plate of vegetable crudités for dipping. If the garlic clove has a green shoot down the centre, remove and discard it, as it can taste very bitter.

Aïoli doesn't keep well. Use it within a few hours of making, or the garlic flavour will become slightly rancid.

1 Peel, smash and finely chop the garlic, then place it in a bowl with the egg yolks.

2 Start to whisk in the oil drop by drop. As the mixture thickens and becomes stable, season with salt and white pepper, then whisk in a tablespoon of the lemon juice. Add a few drops of hot water if it becomes too thick.

3 Whisk in the remaining oil in a thin, steady stream, until you have a thick, glossy mixture. Taste and adjust the seasoning with more lemon juice, salt and pepper.

Inspired by contestant Milla Mackley

Pancetta and Dolcelatte Salad with Parsnip Crisps and Hazelnuts

This salad is a real find. The classic combination of spinach and blue cheese is given a lift by the addition of hazelnuts and parsnip. The dressing holds the salad together and gives it some zest.

→ 1 LARGE PARSNIP, PEELED
→ 100G (4OZ) PANCETTA, SLICED
→ 1 TBSP VEGETABLE OIL
→ 50G (2OZ) BLANCHED HAZELNUTS
→ 225G (8OZ) YOUNG LEAF SPINACH
→ 150G (5OZ) DOLCELATTE CHEESE, CUT INTO SMALL LUMPS

For the dressing:
→ 4 TBSP EXTRA VIRGIN OLIVE OIL
→ 1 SCANT TSP GOOD-QUALITY RED WINE VINEGAR (SUCH AS CABERNET SAUVIGNON)
→ SCANT 1/4 TSP DIJON MUSTARD
→ 1/2 GARLIC CLOVE, CRUSHED
→ A PINCH OF SUGAR
→ A PINCH EACH OF SALT AND PEPPER

1 Preheat the oven to 200°C/400°F/Gas Mark 6.

2 Slice the parsnip very thinly, preferably using a mandoline. Cook in boiling salted water for 30 seconds, then drain well and set aside.

3 Fry the pancetta in a non-stick frying pan until crisp, then drain well, reserving the fat. Stir the vegetable oil and the fat from the pancetta together and use to coat the parsnip slices lightly.

4 Spread the parsnip slices out on a baking tray lined with baking parchment. Place in the oven and cook for about 8 minutes, until crisp and golden brown. Remove from the oven and leave to cool.

5 Put the hazelnuts on a baking sheet and roast for about 5 minutes, until light golden. Remove from the oven and set aside.

6 Place the spinach leaves in a large serving bowl. Put all the ingredients for the dressing into a screw-top jar and shake vigorously to combine. Taste and adjust the seasoning if necessary. Drizzle a little of the dressing over the spinach and toss well, so the leaves are lightly coated.

7 Add the parsnip crisps, pancetta and dolcelatte cheese to the leaves and lightly toss together. Sprinkle the hazelnuts over the salad and serve immediately.

Inspired by contestant Mark Todd

Caesar Salad

Certain dishes are just perfection, whether eaten in New York, Sydney or London. Caesar salad is one of those dishes. However, there are a few things to bear in mind if you want to make it properly. The lettuce must be the crispest and freshest you can find; it should be washed in cold water, dried well and returned to the fridge, then dressed just as you are about to serve it. The croûtons should be well seasoned, soft in the centre, crisp on the outside and definitely not chewy. Now for the dressing – rich and creamy and plenty of it. If you're in any doubt about the amount of dressing, just add more! It can be mopped up with the extra bread that should be served with any great Caesar.

→ 1 COS LETTUCE, LEAVES ROUGHLY TORN
→ 2 LITTLE GEM LETTUCES, LEAVES ROUGHLY TORN
→ 8 ANCHOVY FILLETS
→ A SMALL BLOCK OF PARMESAN CHEESE
For the dressing:
→ 1 EGG YOLK
→ 1 GARLIC CLOVE, CRUSHED
→ JUICE OF ½ LEMON
→ 4 ANCHOVY FILLETS, FINELY CHOPPED
→ 50G (2OZ) PARMESAN CHEESE, FRESHLY GRATED
→ 1 TSP DIJON MUSTARD
→ 4 TBSP LIGHT VEGETABLE OIL
→ 100ML (3½FL OZ) OLIVE OIL
→ A GOOD PINCH OF FRESHLY GROUND BLACK PEPPER
For the croûtons:
→ ½ CIABATTA LOAF, CUT INTO 1CM (½ IN) CUBES
→ 4 TBSP OLIVE OIL
→ 2 TBSP FRESHLY GRATED PARMESAN CHEESE
→ FRESHLY GROUND BLACK PEPPER

1 Preheat the oven to 200ºC/400ºF/Gas Mark 6.

2 For the dressing, place the egg yolk, garlic, lemon juice, anchovies, Parmesan and mustard in a bowl or food processor and mix to a paste. Add the oils a drop at a time, whisking or processing constantly. If the dressing is too thick after all the oil has been added, you can thin it by whisking in a little warm water. Season well with black pepper.

3 For the croûtons, put the bread cubes into a large bowl, drizzle the oil over them and toss together well. Spread the bread out on a baking sheet and sprinkle with the Parmesan and black pepper. Bake for about 8 minutes, until golden brown, then leave to cool.

4 To assemble the salad, put the lettuce and croûtons in a large bowl and toss with the dressing, making sure all the leaves are lightly coated (any leftover dressing will keep in the fridge for 3 days). Garnish with the anchovy fillets. Using a potato peeler, shave the Parmesan over the top, then serve.

Inspired by contestant David Herbert

Autumn Rocket Salad

The thing that makes this salad autumnal is the fact that it is served warm. David wanted to come up with a good, comforting dish. The secret of success is to take your time when cooking the onion, so that it becomes tender and caramelised, in contrast to the crisp pancetta.

→ 100G (4OZ) SMOKED PANCETTA,
  THINLY SLICED
→ 2 TBSP OLIVE OIL
→ 1 LARGE RED ONION, SLICED INTO WEDGES
→ LEAVES FROM 3 SPRIGS OF THYME
→ 100G (4OZ) WILD ROCKET
→ 50G (2OZ) PINE NUTS, TOASTED
→ ½ TSP FRESHLY GROUND BLACK PEPPER
→ 1 TBSP GOOD-QUALITY AGED
  BALSAMIC VINEGAR
→ A SMALL BLOCK OF PARMESAN CHEESE

 MASTERCHEF TOP TIP
Pancetta gets its name from the Italian pancia, meaning belly. It is simply Italian for bacon. Decent British bacon will do the job just as well. Good, dry-cured bacon doesn't sizzle like mad in the pan – only water in hot fat makes that sort of spitting sizzle, and I want fat, not water, in my meat.

One essential bit of advice for making a successful salad: never put anything acidic such as vinegar on to the leaves without first mixing it with oil, otherwise the acid will burn the leaves. Cooked mushy salad leaves are not a good thing. That is why with this salad you should allow the bacon and onion to cool a little before mixing them with the leaves.
Gregg Wallace, Masterchef Judge

1 Heat a non-stick frying pan over a medium heat, add the pancetta and fry for about 3 minutes, turning occasionally, until just crisp. Remove from the pan and set aside.

2 Reduce the heat a little and add the olive oil and onion. Cook slowly for about 10 minutes, stirring frequently, until the onions are beginning to caramelise and soften.

3 Return the pancetta to the pan with the thyme leaves and cook slowly for at least 5 minutes, until the onions are completely tender and the pancetta is crisp and brown. Leave to cool a little.

4 Put the rocket into a salad bowl. Add the still-warm contents of the frying pan, plus the pine nuts, black pepper and balsamic vinegar. Lightly toss everything together. Using a potato peeler, shave the Parmesan over the top, then serve immediately.

Inspired by contestant Alex Baldacci

Warm Salad of Scallops, Black Pudding and Butternut Squash

Scallops and black pudding sound like an unlikely match but they work very well together. They do need some moisture to make them eat well, however. This recipe was cooked on the show without any dressing and it was a little dry. You could either make the dressing given below, or serve it with aïoli (see page 118).

Mashed potato with scallops and black pudding also works a treat, as does some very wet, piping-hot polenta.

→ 50G (2OZ) BUTTER
→ 1 BUTTERNUT SQUASH, PEELED, DESEEDED AND CUT INTO 5CM (2 IN) DICE
→ 2 TBSP LIGHT VEGETABLE OIL, PLUS A LITTLE EXTRA FOR BRUSHING
→ 1 BLACK PUDDING (ABOUT 250G/9OZ), CUT INTO SLICES 1CM (½ IN) THICK
→ 12 KING SCALLOPS
→ SALT AND FRESHLY GROUND BLACK PEPPER
→ LEMON SLICES AND SNIPPED CHIVES, TO GARNISH
For the dressing:
→ 4 TBSP EXTRA VIRGIN OLIVE OIL
→ 4 TBSP GROUNDNUT OIL
→ A PINCH OF SEA SALT
→ A PINCH OF WHITE PEPPER
→ 1 TBSP GOOD-QUALITY WHITE WINE VINEGAR
→ 2 TSP LEMON JUICE
→ 1 TBSP SNIPPED CHIVES

Ⓜ **MASTERCHEF TOP TIP**
Buy good-quality scallops, preferably diver-caught ones, that have not been frozen and do not wash them – just wipe them clean with a dry cloth.
John Torode, Masterchef Judge

1 Put the butter, squash, 100ml (3½fl oz) water and some salt and pepper in a medium pan and bring to the boil. Simmer for 10 minutes or until the squash is tender, then strain off any excess liquid and reserve.

2 Mash the squash and adjust the seasoning. If the squash is dry, add a little of the reserved cooking liquid. Reheat gently, stirring constantly, until thick and smooth. Remove from the heat and keep warm.

3 Heat the oil in a frying pan and gently fry the black pudding in it until crisp. Remove from the pan and keep warm.

4 Lightly brush a ridged griddle pan or a heavy-based frying pan with a little oil and place it over a high heat until very hot. Season the scallops with a little salt, place them in the hot pan and sear for 1 minute on each side, until browned and lightly caramelised. Remove from the pan.

5 For the dressing, put all the ingredients in a bowl and whisk together until emulsified.

6 Place a good spoonful of the squash purée on 4 serving plates. Arrange the scallops and black pudding slices in overlapping layers on each plate and garnish with lemon slices. Drizzle the dressing over the warm scallop salad and serve immediately, sprinkled with snipped chives. (Any leftover dressing can be stored in the fridge for 2–3 days.)

Minted Prawn Salad

The combination of mint, parsley and coriander is not a new one. The Vietnamese have long used it to add freshness to salads and soups, which often contain sour flavours. Don't overcook the prawns, and serve this salad as soon as it is ready, otherwise it will go soggy and be unpleasant to eat.

→ 1 SMALL PARSNIP, SLICED ABOUT 2MM (1/12 IN) THICK
→ 4 TBSP VEGETABLE OIL
→ 550G (1¼LB) LARGE, HEADLESS RAW PRAWNS, SHELL ON
→ 200G (7OZ) BABY SALAD LEAVES
→ A HANDFUL OF FRESH CORIANDER, CHOPPED
→ 2 SPRIGS OF MINT, CHOPPED
→ A SPRIG OF FLAT-LEAF PARSLEY, CHOPPED
→ SALT AND FRESHLY GROUND BLACK PEPPER

For the dressing:
→ 1 SMALL, MILD RED CHILLI, FINELY CHOPPED
→ GRATED ZEST OF 1 LIME
→ 1 TABLESPOON LIME JUICE
→ 2 TBSP SOFT LIGHT BROWN SUGAR
→ 2 TBSP THAI FISH SAUCE (NAM PLA)
→ 4 TABLESPOONS LIGHT VEGETABLE OIL
→ A FEW DROPS OF SESAME OIL

1 Preheat the oven to 200°C/400°F/Gas Mark 6.

2 Cook the parsnip slices in boiling salted water until tender, then drain well and dry on kitchen paper. Spread out on a baking sheet and brush with a little of the vegetable oil. Bake for about 15 minutes, until crisp, then set aside.

3 Meanwhile, prepare the prawns by peeling off the shells, leaving the last tail segment in place. If the intestinal tract that runs down the back of each prawn is visible, remove it with the point of a sharp knife. Season the prawns and toss them in the remaining oil, then set aside.

4 For the dressing, place the chopped chilli in a bowl with the lime zest and juice. Whisk in the sugar, fish sauce, vegetable oil and sesame oil.

5 Heat a large, heavy-based frying pan over a high heat, tip the prawns into the pan and sear for 2 minutes on each side. Do not be tempted to shake the pan as they cook. When they are pink and cooked through, remove them from the pan and mix with the parsnip crisps. Fold in a little of the dressing.

6 Put the salad leaves on 4 serving plates and top with the prawn mixture. Mix the fresh herbs together and sprinkle them on top. Drizzle more dressing over the salad and serve immediately.

'I like the punch of the prawns and the dressing.'
John Torode, Masterchef Judge

Warm Salad of Partridge Breast, Jerusalem Artichokes, Walnuts and Watercress

Ah, the flavours of autumn! Simply roasted partridge with peppery watercress, walnuts and nutty Jerusalem artichokes – this salad really is the bee's knees. But beware – it must be served as soon as it is mixed, and preferably while the birds are still warm, or it can be a little dry.

→ 4 PLUMP PARTRIDGES
→ 50G (2OZ) BUTTER
→ 4 TBSP QUINCE JAM OR GOOD-QUALITY AROMATIC HONEY
→ 2 TBSP VEGETABLE OIL
→ 1 TSP LEMON JUICE
→ 400G (14OZ) SMALL JERUSALEM ARTICHOKES, PEELED
→ 2 TBSP EXTRA VIRGIN OLIVE OIL
→ 200G (7OZ) WATERCRESS
→ 100G (4OZ) WALNUT HALVES
→ SALT AND FRESHLY GROUND BLACK PEPPER

For the dressing:
→ 6 TBSP EXTRA VIRGIN OLIVE OIL
→ ½ TSP DIJON MUSTARD
→ 2 TSP RED WINE VINEGAR

1 Preheat the oven to 200°C/400°F/Gas Mark 6.

2 Season the birds inside and out with salt and pepper. Divide the butter into 4 pieces and put them into the cavities of the birds with the quince jam or honey. Place the birds upside down in a roasting tin. Spoon the vegetable oil over them and rub it into the skin. Roast for about 20 minutes, until cooked through, then remove from the oven and leave to rest in a warm place.

3 Meanwhile, add the lemon juice to a saucepan of boiling water and then add the artichokes. Simmer until just cooked but still firm, then drain.

4 Preheat a ridged griddle pan. Toss the artichokes with the olive oil, then chargrill just long enough for them to catch a little colour. Remove from the heat and keep warm.

5 Make the dressing by whisking all the ingredients together with salt and pepper to taste.

6 Put the watercress leaves and walnuts in a large bowl and toss with just enough dressing to coat the leaves lightly. Arrange on a large salad plate. Remove the warm breast meat from the birds, slice it and arrange over the salad leaves, together with the chargrilled artichokes. Serve immediately, while the meat and artichokes are still warm.

'Thomasina has produced food that is interesting, exciting and delicious.'
John Torode, Masterchef Judge

Inspired by contestant Tim Loo

Salad of Honey- and Soy-roasted Duck Breast, Orange and Radicchio

This clever little salad uses a distinctive sweet and sour approach. Start the duck breasts off in a cold pan, so that the fat will melt slowly from under the skin.

→ 4 LARGE DUCK BREASTS
→ 3 TBSP HONEY
→ 2 TBSP SOY SAUCE
→ A GOOD PINCH OF WHITE PEPPER
→ 3 ORANGES
→ 1–2 RADICCHIO HEADS
→ A GOOD HANDFUL OF CHIVES, SNIPPED
For the dressing:
→ 1 TSP GOOD-QUALITY BALSAMIC VINEGAR
→ 1 TSP SESAME OIL
→ A PINCH OF CASTER SUGAR

1 With a sharp knife, score (but don't cut through) the skin of the duck in a criss-cross pattern about 1cm (½ in) apart.

2 Mix the honey, soy sauce and white pepper in a large dish. Add the duck breasts, skin-side down, and marinate for 15 minutes. Turn the duck over and marinate for a further 15 minutes.

3 Peel the oranges with a sharp knife, cutting away all the white pith. Over a bowl to catch the juice, cut away the orange segments from between the membranes. When you have finished, squeeze out the juice from the membrane into the bowl. Set the bowl of orange juice and the orange segments to one side. Tear the radicchio leaves apart and place in a bowl of cold water.

4 Preheat the oven to 180°C/350°F/Gas Mark 4. Remove the duck breasts from the marinade and pat dry with kitchen paper. Place an ovenproof frying pan on the hob, put the duck breasts into the cold pan, skin-side down, and heat slowly, increasing the heat gradually until the duck is frying. Cook for 12–15 minutes, until the skin is well coloured and slightly crisp, then turn the duck breasts over and drain away any excess fat.

5 Transfer the pan to the oven and cook for 6 minutes. Remove from the oven. Turn the breasts over, draining away excess fat.

6 Place the pan on the hob and sear the duck over a high heat for 5–6 minutes to crisp the skin. Remove from the heat and leave to rest in a warm place.

7 Mix the dressing ingredients together with 50ml (2fl oz) of the reserved orange juice and taste. If it is too sharp, add a little more orange juice.

8 Mix the orange segments, drained radicchio leaves and chives together in a bowl. Cut the duck breasts into thin slices and arrange over the salad. Pour the dressing on top and serve.

Inspired by contestant Mark Rigby

Carpaccio with Rocket

Beef carpaccio – what a beauty! This was first served at Harry's Bar in Venice, and was named after the Renaissance Venetian painter. If you are not used to it, you may find the texture of raw beef a little strange but I love it. A good Caesar-style dressing also works well here. Serve with warm bread.

→ 400G (14OZ) BEST-QUALITY BEEF FILLET, WELL TRIMMED OF ANY FAT
→ JUICE OF ½ LEMON
→ 4 TBSP EXTRA VIRGIN OLIVE OIL
→ A LARGE HANDFUL OF ROCKET LEAVES
→ A SMALL BLOCK OF PARMESAN CHEESE
→ SALT AND FRESHLY GROUND BLACK PEPPER

MASTERCHEF TOP TIP
Carpaccio must be made with beef fillet that has been well hung to mature it. Before cutting the meat, roll it very tightly in cling film, then chill it as much as possible without actually freezing it. This will give a good round shape and will make cutting thin slices much easier. As an alternative way of serving it, you could briefly deep-fry the rocket, sprinkle with toasted sesame seeds and extra virgin olive oil, and serve with hot olive, sage and onion bread.
Peter Richards, Masterchef Mentor

1 Using a very sharp knife, cut the beef into paper-thin slices. Lay the slices between 2 sheets of greaseproof paper and flatten with a meat mallet or a rolling pin – the thinner the better.

2 Whisk the lemon juice and oil together to make a dressing.

3 Lightly season the rocket with salt and pepper. Scatter the rocket over a serving platter and arrange the beef slices on top.

4 Brush the beef with the dressing. Using a potato peeler, shave the Parmesan over the beef slices. Serve with warm bread.

'I want to get through to the next stage... I want to get to the end... I want to win it!'
Mark Rigby, Contestant

Masterchef Masterclass
John Torode's Egg Basics

In the UK we consume nearly 30 million eggs a day, yet for something so fundamental to our diet we seem to know very little about how to cook them. Isn't it time we stopped taking eggs for granted and began to appreciate them more? Beautifully encased in their pristine shells, eggs are the perfect nutritional package: an excellent source of protein, vitamins and iron. In culinary terms, their uses are astonishingly varied: they can be boiled, baked, fried, scrambled, poached or made into omelettes. They form the basis of soufflés, custards, batters, meringues, and sauces such as hollandaise and mayonnaise. And they have an important role in enriching, thickening and binding sweet and savoury dishes.

Few of us nowadays are privileged enough to have a few hens out the back but we can still try to buy eggs that are as fresh as possible. Buy organic if you can – the birds will have been kept fairly and not subjected to undue stress. Furthermore, they will have been fed a good diet that doesn't include routine antibiotics. The colour of the shell has no effect on the flavour of the egg, it is simply a result of the breed of hen.

You can test how fresh an egg is by placing it in a bowl of water: if the egg lays flat, it is fresh; if it starts to stand up, or even floats, it is time for it to go in the bin.

Another way of testing for freshness is to break an egg on to a plate: the white should be jelly-like and hold the yolk up in a well-formed mound. If the white is watery and the yolk flat, the egg is old – still usable but best for baking.

All eggs that are to be eaten hot should be served as soon as they are ready. The white and yolk are made primarily of protein, which changes in colour and form when you apply heat to it. In the case of a boiled egg in particular, it will continue to cook when taken from the heat. This is why you sometimes end up with a hard-boiled egg when you are convinced it should be soft.

John Torode's
Basic Boiled Egg

Eggs that are a few days old are best for boiling. As the egg ages, natural gases accumulate between the shell and the fine membrane holding the white. A fresh egg will be harder to peel. The timings given below are for medium eggs.

Boiled eggs to be served hot

Place the eggs in a pan with plenty of room for them to move around. Fill with cold water and place over a high heat. Bring just to the boil, then reduce to a simmer (this will stop the eggs bashing into each other). Once simmering, for soft-boiled eggs, cook for 3 minutes, then remove from the heat and serve immediately, with toast soldiers, a large knob of butter, and some salt and pepper. For hard-boiled eggs, cook for $4\frac{1}{2}$–5 minutes.

Boiled eggs to be served cold

For the perfect soft-boiled salad egg, bring a pan of water to the boil, gently lower in the eggs and return to the boil. Reduce the heat to a simmer and cook for exactly $4\frac{1}{2}$ minutes. Lift the eggs from the water, place in a bowl of cold water and run water from the tap over the top until they are cool. Keep them immersed in the water when peeling, to prevent them breaking up, and store them in fresh water if you are not using them straight away. For hard-boiled eggs, increase the cooking time to $5\frac{1}{2}$ minutes.

John Torode's
Basic Poached Egg

Very fresh eggs are best for poaching. Take the largest, deepest pan you can find and fill it with boiling water from the kettle (you may need to boil the kettle several times). For every litre of water, add 3 tablespoons of white wine vinegar. Bring the water to a rolling boil, then reduce the heat to a simmer. Break each egg into the water slowly (you can use a bowl or cup if you're nervous), so that the egg white sets before hitting the base of the pan; as it falls, it should form a teardrop shape, then wrap itself round into a nice oval. If you are using a 5-litre (9-pint) pan you can cook up to 8 eggs at a time. Keep the water moving by raising the heat a little with every few eggs you add.

Each egg will take 2 minutes once it has floated to the top. Gently lift it from the water with a slotted spoon. You can keep the eggs in a bowl of cold water, to be reheated in a pan of boiling water later if you wish. Alternatively, place on kitchen paper to drain, then serve straight away.

John Torode's
Basic Fried Egg

I love my fried eggs with crisp edges. Heat about 2 tablespoons of oil, preferably olive oil, in a non-stick frying pan until it is quite hot, then drop the egg in and let it start to spit and splutter – that is all part of the plan. Reduce the heat to low so the yolk sets, then right at the last minute turn the heat up to full and cook for 30 seconds. There you have it: crispy-edged fried egg, fantastic on hot buttered toast. But then you knew that already.

John Torode's
Basic Scrambled Eggs

Salt is the raw egg's enemy: it breaks down the white and makes it sloppy. When making scrambled eggs, I add the salt and pepper to the butter as it is melting in the pan, rather than to the eggs.

If scrambled eggs are overcooked they become watery, because the protein has been destroyed so that it can no longer hold the water. This makes the toast soggy and the eggs taste slightly tinny, rather than rich and creamy.

For 2 people, crack 5 eggs into a bowl and puncture the yolks with a fork, but do not whisk. Stir in 3 tablespoons of double cream. Heat a heavy-based pan over a medium heat and add 100g (4oz) butter, plus a good pinch of salt and a couple of turns from the pepper mill. When the butter has nearly all melted, add the eggs and reduce the heat to low. Stir with a wooden spoon in one direction only, ensuring that none of the egg sticks to the bottom of the pan. When it looks like thick, lumpy custard, remove the pan from the heat and stir a little more while the toast cooks. Butter the toast and serve the scrambled eggs on top.

Name: Rachel Szadura
Age: 39
Occupation: Trying 24-7 to get on television, cooking!
Place of residence: Bakewell, Derbyshire
Why did you apply to Masterchef?
Because I felt that as a true foodie and someone who's extremely passionate, I thought I had what it takes to win the competition.
What do you cook at home and who do you cook for?
I'm constantly entertaining – we have friends round all the time. I mostly cook English, Italian and Indian food. I have a large circle of friends and they often take 40- or 50-mile detours to come to my house because they know I'll always be knocking something up in the kitchen. Believe you me, I'm the real domestic goddess.
What is your favourite meal?
I couldn't possibly say: I have too many favourites!
What are your aspirations in the world of cooking and food?
I want to be on television cooking and be known to the whole nation as 'the Kitten in the Kitchen'! I would also love to meet Gordon Ramsay – he would meet his match. And I'd love to be the face of a major food retailer – just like Jamie Oliver!

Name: Scott Ball
Age: 32
Occupation: Computer and business consultant.
Place of residence: East London
Why did you apply to Masterchef?
I really love food – I'm not a petite flower! I've always had a passion for food and a passion for cooking and I thought it would be a great avenue for furthering my cooking skills.
What do you cook at home and who do you cook for?
I cook for my partner and friends and I cook everything! I'm a bit of a crazy chef. I'm inspired by ingredients. I'm also a keen gardener, so I grow a lot of my own fruit and vegetables on my allotment and I have a passion for the whole cycle from growing to cooking. I particularly love modern comfort foods; most are simple yet decadent at the same time.
What is your favourite meal?
Sausage and mash, because it's good, hardy, filling, simplistic food. If you have great sausages, they make a fantastic meal.
What are your aspirations in the world of cooking and food?
Some day I would really like to either open a restaurant or a gourmet food shop, getting the food and delivering the right ingredients to people.

Name: Thomasina Miers
Age: 28
Occupation: I'm currently compiling a cookbook that will be published next September.
Place of residence: West London
Why did you apply to Masterchef?
I was in Ireland, staying on a cheese farm I used to work at, looking at some magazines, and saw an article on the series and filled in the application form for fun. I never dreamed that anyone would call me up.
What do you cook at home and who do you cook for?
I cook for my friends all the time, and I cook pretty much everything. I live near some great Middle Eastern produce shops, so I cook a lot of food from that region. I live with an Italian chef, so we cook a lot of Italian too. I also cook Mexican food – I worked in Mexico helping some people to set up a restaurant and bar, and toured around Mexico for two months; I love experimenting with new flavours.
What is your favourite meal?
I love eating everything! I love Spanish food and I love chorizo with anything.
What are your aspirations in the world of cooking and food?
I guess it would always be to learn more and inspire other people with what I've learned. There's so much I want to do.

Inspired by contestant Caroline Brewester

Gougère with Mushrooms in Marsala Sauce

As with asparagus in May, when wild mushrooms come into season in autumn, we get such a limited time to eat them that it's tempting to gorge ourselves!

- → 25G (1OZ) BUTTER
- → 2 SHALLOTS, FINELY CHOPPED
- → 1 GARLIC CLOVE, FINELY CHOPPED
- → 400G (14OZ) MUSHROOMS (A MIXTURE OF WILD AND CHESTNUT MUSHROOMS), SLICED
- → 1 TBSP CHOPPED FLAT-LEAF PARSLEY
- → SALT AND FRESHLY GROUND BLACK PEPPER

For the choux pastry:
- → 100G (4OZ) PLAIN FLOUR
- → A PINCH OF SALT
- → A PINCH OF CAYENNE PEPPER
- → 75G (3OZ) BUTTER, DICED
- → 3 EGGS, BEATEN
- → 25G (1OZ) GRUYÈRE CHEESE, GRATED
- → 25G (1OZ) PARMESAN CHEESE, FINELY GRATED

For the marsala sauce:
- → 15G (½OZ) BUTTER
- → 1 LARGE SHALLOT, FINELY CHOPPED
- → 100ML (3½FL OZ) DRY MARSALA
- → 250ML (8FL OZ) DOUBLE CREAM

For the watercress salad:
- → 100G (4OZ) WATERCRESS
- → 2–3 TSP OLIVE OIL
- → 1 TSP LEMON JUICE

1 Preheat the oven to 200°C/400°F/Gas Mark 6.

2 To make the choux pastry, sift the flour, salt and cayenne pepper into a bowl and set aside. Put the butter and 215 ml (7½ fl oz) water in a small, heavy-based saucepan. Heat gently, then bring to a full boil. Remove from the heat and immediately drop in all the seasoned flour. Whisk vigorously until the mixture leaves the side of the pan. Cool slightly, then whisk in the beaten egg a little at a time, using a hand-held electric beater and whisking well after each addition. You may not need all the egg; the mixture should have a fairly firm dropping consistency. Carry on beating until the paste has a definite sheen, then beat in the cheese.

3 Grease 2 large baking trays. Pile 2 high mounds of the mixture on to each tray to make 4 large buns, leaving room for them to spread. Bake in 2 batches for 30 minutes. Do not open the oven door during the cooking time or they will collapse.

4 Remove the buns from the oven when they are dark golden and crisp. Cut off a lid from each bun and set aside. Scrape out any wet paste with a teaspoon and discard. Keep the buns warm.

5 For the marsala sauce, melt the butter in a small frying pan, add the shallot and fry over a medium heat until soft and translucent. Pour in the marsala and simmer until reduced by half. Stir in the cream and simmer until reduced by half again. Season to taste, then remove from the heat, cover and keep warm.

6 To make the filling, melt the butter in a large frying pan, add the shallots and garlic and fry until soft and translucent. Add the mushrooms and sauté until tender. Pour the marsala sauce over the mushroom mixture and stir lightly to combine. Gently stir in the parsley, then taste and adjust the seasoning.

7 Place the choux buns on 4 plates, pile the mushroom mixture into them and top with the reserved lids. Toss the watercress with the olive oil and lemon juice, season, and serve with the buns.

Inspired by contestant Christopher Souto

Leek and Wild Mushroom
Vol-au-vents with Watercress Coulis

People tend to be snobbish about vol-au-vents because they are a throwback to the seventies, when there were a lot of badly made ones about. In fact, they make great party food. The pastry cases can be prepared in advance, then filled and reheated to serve piping hot. You can make them any size you like – as a nibble or, as in this recipe, as a starter.

→ 350G (12OZ) PUFF PASTRY
→ 1 EGG, LIGHTLY BEATEN
→ 2 TBSP OLIVE OIL
→ 250G (9OZ) LEEKS, SLICED
   INTO JULIENNE (FINE SHREDS)
→ 1 GARLIC CLOVE, FINELY CHOPPED
→ 150G (5OZ) MIXED WILD
   MUSHROOMS, SLICED
→ 3 SPRIGS OF LEMON THYME
→ 10G (¼OZ) BUTTER
→ 2 TSP PLAIN FLOUR
→ 100ML (3½FL OZ) DOUBLE CREAM
→ SALT AND FRESHLY GROUND
   BLACK PEPPER
   For the watercress coulis:
→ 75G (3OZ) CHARLOTTE POTATOES, PEELED
→ 75G (3OZ) WATERCRESS, STALKS REMOVED
→ 2–4 TBSP VEGETABLE STOCK

1 Preheat the oven to 200°C/400°F/Gas Mark 6.

2 Roll out the pastry until it is 5mm (¼ in) thick, then cut out 4 rounds, using a 9cm (3½ in) plain cutter. Place the rounds on a dampened baking sheet. Using a 7.5cm (3 in) plain cutter, cut part way through the centre of each round. Prick the inner circle with a fork and brush the outer circle with a little of the beaten egg. Chill for 20 minutes.

3 Bake for 10 minutes or until well risen and golden brown. Carefully remove the centre lids and keep warm.

4 For the watercress coulis, thinly slice the potatoes, preferably using a mandoline. Put the slices in a small saucepan of boiling salted water and simmer until they just start to soften and lose their raw flavour. Drain and set aside.

5 Put the watercress in a colander and pour over enough boiling water for it to wilt but not lose its vibrant colour. Purée the potato and watercress with 2 tablespoons of vegetable stock, then put through a fine sieve. Loosen the coulis with a little more vegetable stock, if necessary, then set aside.

6 Heat a tablespoon of the olive oil in a small pan, add the leeks and garlic, then cover and sweat for 5–6 minutes, until soft. Remove from the heat and set aside.

'I used to say (to the contestants) "work smart, not hard". If you work intelligently you don't have to work hard – you think your way through things.'
Peter Richards, Masterchef Mentor

7 Heat the remaining olive oil in a frying pan. Add the mushrooms and the leaves from the thyme sprigs and cook until the mushrooms are almost tender. Remove from the heat and set aside.

8 Melt the butter in a small saucepan over a low heat. Stir in the flour and mix to a paste, then cook gently for 1 minute. Add the cream and stir constantly over a low heat until the sauce thickens. Remove from the heat.

9 Mix the leeks and three-quarters of the mushrooms together. Stir in the white sauce and season to taste.

10 Generously fill the cavity of the vol-au-vents with the leek and mushroom mixture and place on 4 serving plates. Cover with the pastry lids. Scatter the reserved mushrooms around them and drizzle the watercress coulis over the plates. Serve immediately.

Masterchef Masterclass
John Torode's Omelette

Almost everybody makes omelettes but unfortunately very few people make them well. They should be cooked slowly in a generous amount of butter and seasoned well with white pepper rather than black. They should be soft and slightly runny – or baveuse, as the French call it – and have very little colour on the outside. They should look thick and sumptuous, like a soft pillow. And they should be served hot. Most of the time, omelettes are served in completely the opposite fashion, as horrid, hard, overcooked slabs of egg.

Flat omelettes, such as the Spanish tortilla and the Italian frittata, are a different thing altogether from the classic omelette – and, though I admit I'm partisan, as far away from a beautiful, soft omelette as a Robin Reliant is from a classic sports car.

A good omelette takes practice but it is worth it. Keep it simple, follow the tips below, and don't start experimenting with fillings until you have mastered the basic plain version.

→ The correct pan is vital for cooking omelettes. It should be made of cast iron, preferably with a non-stick surface, and should have sloping sides so you can slide the omelette out easily. For a 3-egg omelette you will need an 18cm (7 in) pan.

→ Use really good, fresh eggs and butter, so the omelette is well flavoured rather than bland.

→ Beat the eggs thoroughly before cooking, to give an even, homogeneous mixture.

→ Be sure to cook the omelette at the correct heat level: too high and it will be tough and dry; too low and it will be flat and more like scrambled egg. The entire cooking time shouldn't be more than 3–4 minutes.

→ Remember that the omelette will continue to cook in its own heat after you take it off the hob, so make sure the mixture is still slightly runny in the centre.

→ Always serve omelettes straight away, on a hot plate, so they don't cool down and become tough.

John Torode's
Basic Omelette

SERVES 1
→ 3 LARGE EGGS
→ 2 TEASPOONS DOUBLE CREAM
  (OPTIONAL)
→ 50G (2OZ) BUTTER
→ SALT AND WHITE PEPPER

1 Break the eggs into a mixing bowl and add the cream, if using. Mix well with a fork, then season with salt and pepper.

2 Place an omelette pan over a medium heat and add the butter. When it is melted and starting to foam, reduce the heat and pour in the egg. Gently move it around with a fork for a few seconds so it starts to cook evenly.

3 Using the fork, draw back the set egg around the edges and tilt the pan, so the uncooked egg flows out to the sides. Cook for a few seconds longer, until the underneath is lightly coloured but the top still moist.

4 Raise the pan, as if you were showing someone the contents, but leave the far end resting on the hob. Using a spatula or a fork, ease the raised end of the omelette over so it starts to roll. Fold the omelette over and tip it on to a warm plate. Serve immediately.

Fillings
Fillings that don't need cooking, such as chopped herbs or grated cheese, can be added just before you fold the omelette; the cheese will start to melt in the heat of the eggs. Fillings such as mushrooms or bacon should be cooked in a separate pan, then added to the omelette before folding.

Posh Mushrooms on Toast

This dish makes a wonderful starter. It calls for a good-sized glass of robust red wine to go with it. At the beginning of autumn, wild mushrooms are readily available and many are from the UK.

→ 1 TBSP OLIVE OIL
→ 50G (2OZ) SMOKED PANCETTA, DICED
→ 1–2 GARLIC CLOVES, FINELY CHOPPED
→ 25G (1OZ) UNSALTED BUTTER
→ 200G (7OZ) MIXED WILD MUSHROOMS
  (SUCH AS CHANTERELLES, CEPS AND
  MORELS), CUT IN HALF IF LARGE
→ 3 TBSP DRY WHITE WINE
→ 3 TBSP ROUGHLY CHOPPED FLAT-LEAF
  PARSLEY
→ 4 SLICES OF SOURDOUGH BREAD
  OR SIMILAR
→ SALT AND FRESHLY GROUND
  BLACK PEPPER

1 Heat the oil in a large frying pan, add the pancetta and fry until golden brown, stirring occasionally. Add the garlic and cook over a low heat until soft and translucent.

2 Raise the heat a little and add a small knob of the butter. When it starts to foam, stir in the mushrooms and cook for 2–3 minutes.

3 Add the wine and let it bubble until almost evaporated. Season with plenty of salt and pepper, stir in the parsley and set aside.

4 Toast the bread on a ridged griddle pan or under the grill. Use the remaining butter to spread on the toast. Top with the mushroom mixture and serve immediately.

MASTERCHEF TOP TIP

If you ever go foraging for mushrooms, never, and I mean NEVER, eat anything you don't recognise. Some fungi are extremely poisonous. On the other hand, buying wild mushrooms from food shops is as safe as a very safe thing on National Safe Day! Some packs of wild mushrooms contain cultivated 'wild' varieties – oyster and shiitake, for example. I don't know about you, but I don't think wild means farmed! To clean mushrooms, gently remove the dirt with a soft brush. Don't wash them, or they will get waterlogged and become slimy when cooked.
Gregg Wallace, Masterchef Judge

'John, you're a judge, not the Spanish Inquisition!'
Gregg Wallace, Masterchef Judge

Masterchef Masterclass
John Torode's Tomato Sauce

The simplest and best sauce for pasta is a well-seasoned, beautifully cooked tomato sauce. The most successful way to make it is not with fresh tomatoes but with canned ones, which will have been picked when ripe and preserved in a good amount of their own juice.

Tomatoes first appeared in Italy in the late sixteenth century but it wasn't until the eighteenth century that they became widely used in cooking. In the early nineteenth century, an enterprising Neapolitan company started canning local tomatoes for export, and this is still the best way to taste a true Italian tomato outside Italy. Top-quality canned tomatoes are sweet, with a good flesh-to-seed ratio, and keep their deep-red colour even after being subjected to the high heat used by the canning industry. Most of the fresh tomatoes on offer in supermarkets have been selected for their looks rather than their taste. They are quick-growing varieties, developed to have thick skins so they have a long shelf life and don't bruise easily. Tomatoes labelled 'vine-ripened' tend to be superior but you pay a premium for them.

I have one little thing to whinge about. I don't understand why people dismember a fresh tomato in the name of culinary art. They blanch them, skin them, cut them into quarters, remove the seeds and then cut the sodden flesh into little squares. Do they really think little squares of boiled tomato taste nice?

It's cheaper, quicker and more convenient to use canned tomatoes for pasta sauces. It will also give a much better result, especially if you follow the tips below:

→ Buy good-quality Italian canned tomatoes, as some cheaper brands contain a lot of water.
→ Don't boil the sauce rapidly, or it will evaporate too quickly and become bitter and solid.
→ Cooking gently is the key, and stirring well so the sauce does not stick to the bottom of the pan.
→ Mix the sauce thoroughly with hot pasta immediately before serving. It should be shiny from the olive oil and not sticky at all.

John Torode's
Basic Tomato Sauce

MAKES ENOUGH FOR 500G (1LB 2OZ) PASTA

→ 4 TBSP OLIVE OIL
→ 1 ONION, DICED
→ 1 GARLIC CLOVE, CRUSHED
→ 1 TSP SEA SALT
→ 1 TSP FRESHLY GROUND BLACK PEPPER
→ 2 X 400G (14OZ) CANS OF CHOPPED TOMATOES
→ CHOPPED BASIL AND FRESHLY GRATED PARMESAN CHEESE, TO SERVE

1 Heat the oil in a heavy-based pan over a moderate heat. Add the onion and cook, stirring constantly, for 3 minutes, until softened. Add the garlic, salt and pepper and cook for 2 minutes.

2 Add the tomatoes and bring to the boil. Reduce the heat to a simmer and cook for 6–8 minutes, stirring occasionally, until the sauce is slightly thickened.

3 Take off the heat and toss with freshly cooked pasta. Serve sprinkled with chopped fresh basil and Parmesan cheese.

4 If you don't want to use the sauce straight away, it will keep, covered, in the fridge for a week, or in the freezer for about 3 months. You can also adapt it to use on pizzas by cooking it for about 10 minutes longer, until it has thickened and most of the juices have evaporated.

Inspired by contestant Shel Musiker

Goat's Cheese and Red Onion Tarts

Goat's cheese and red onions always work a treat together. The great thing about these tarts is that they fit into any season – try taking them on a picnic in the summer sun, or eat them hot for a winter supper. They also make a wonderful vegetarian dish.

- → 375G (13OZ) PUFF PASTRY
- → 50G (2OZ) BUTTER
- → 2 LARGE RED ONIONS, THINLY SLICED
- → A FEW SPRIGS OF THYME
- → 1 TSP WHITE WINE VINEGAR
- → 175G (6OZ) GOAT'S CHEESE LOG,
  CUT INTO THIN SLICES
- → 1 SMALL EGG, LIGHTLY BEATEN
- → SALT AND FRESHLY
  GROUND BLACK PEPPER

1 Preheat the oven to 220°C/425°F/Gas Mark 7.

2 Roll the pastry out to about 5mm (¼ in) thick. Cut out four 15cm (6 in) rounds, using a small plate as a guide. Place the rounds of pastry on a lightly greased baking sheet. Using a sharp knife, mark a 1cm (½ in) rim around the edge of the pastry, making sure you don't cut right through it. Lightly prick the area inside the rim with a fork. Chill for 30 minutes.

3 Melt the butter in a heavy-based frying pan over a medium heat. Add the onions and thyme and cook, stirring frequently, for 4–5 minutes. Add the vinegar, reduce the heat and cook until the onions are soft. Remove from the heat, discard the thyme and leave to cool.

4 Divide the onion mixture between the pastry bases, leaving the rim free. Top with the goat's cheese slices and season with salt and pepper.

5 Lightly brush the rim of the pastry with beaten egg. Bake for 15–20 minutes, until the pastry is well risen and golden brown. Remove from the oven and serve immediately.

Masterchef Masterclass
John Torode's Risotto

There is something wonderfully comforting about a risotto. It is warming, creamy and filling, and when cooked well it is one of the most delicious dishes in the world. The classic risottos are the best, as the simpler the flavours the more intense the end product.

To make a great risotto, you need patience and time. Not a great deal of time, though – say, 40 minutes in total, with 20 minutes of that going on the preparation and 20 minutes on the cooking. You also need to devote your attention to it fully while it cooks, stirring it almost constantly and maintaining a consistent heat level. You will be rewarded with that unique creamy texture, with each grain of rice tender yet still slightly firm in the centre.

Risotto is made with just a handful of ingredients but they must be of good quality. The rice in particular is paramount. Italian short grain rice, grown in the north of the country, is uniquely suited to risotto. It can absorb a great deal of liquid during cooking without breaking up, and it is high in starch, which dissolves into the liquid and thickens it. Arborio is the best-known variety, while the slightly more expensive carnaroli and vialone nano are becoming increasingly available in this country.

'Did you know that you should only ever stir risotto in one direction? . . . All the grains roll together and in doing so they never break up.'
John Torode, Masterchef Judge

No matter how you flavour a risotto, the basic technique is the same every time. Here are the essential steps for success:

→ Choose a heavy-based pan that is large enough to allow the rice to swell by about three times its volume.

→ The flavour base of most risottos consists of finely chopped shallot sweated in butter and/or oil. Keep the heat low at this stage, so the shallot becomes soft and translucent but does not colour. Then add the rice and stir it around for a few minutes until it is coated in the fat; this will prevent it sticking.

→ Keep the stock at simmering point in a separate pan so the temperature of the rice doesn't drop when you add it. Otherwise, the rice may be cooked on the outside before it is ready on the inside.

→ Add the stock a ladleful at a time, stirring constantly and letting it be absorbed by the rice before you add more. Be careful not to beat the mixture. Just stir it gently and carefully, scraping it up from the base of the pan, so the rice absorbs the liquid evenly. Do this over a moderate heat; the rice should be ticking over at a gentle simmer. If the heat is too high, the rice will move around too much and break up; if it is too low, the rice will become glutinous and heavy.

→ The cooking time from the moment you add the rice should be 15–20 minutes. When the risotto is done, it should be neither stiff nor runny, with the rice lightly bound together yet the grains still separate.

→ The classic way to finish a risotto is by vigorously beating butter and Parmesan into it to enrich it. This is known as the *mantecatura*.

→ Finally, always serve risotto straight away. It becomes stodgy if it is kept waiting.

'It's comfort food, it's wonderful food . . . and the good thing about a risotto is that it will absorb so many other flavours.'
Gregg Wallace, Masterchef Judge

John Torode's
Wild Mushroom Risotto

SERVES 4
- → ABOUT 3 TBSP OLIVE OIL
- → 4 SHALLOTS, FINELY DICED
- → 4 GARLIC CLOVES, CRUSHED
- → ABOUT 500G (1LB 2OZ) MIXED WILD MUSHROOMS, SUCH AS CHANTERELLES, PIEDS DE MOUTON, WOOD BLEWITS AND PORCINI, CLEANED
- → A HANDFUL OF PARSLEY, CHOPPED
- → 1 LITRE (1¾ PINTS) GOOD-QUALITY CHICKEN STOCK
- → 15G (½OZ) BUTTER, PLUS A GOOD KNOB OF BUTTER FOR FINISHING
- → A HANDFUL OF DRIED PORCINI MUSHROOMS
- → 340G (12OZ) ARBORIO RICE
- → 100G (4OZ) PARMESAN CHEESE, FRESHLY GRATED
- → SALT AND FRESHLY GROUND BLACK PEPPER

This risotto contains both dried and fresh wild mushrooms. Half the dried mushrooms are ground into a powder, then added to the risotto at the end – a simple but effective idea, whereby the intense, concentrated flavour of the porcini acts as a substitute for salt.

If you ever get your hands on some fresh truffles, you can be really indulgent and shave them over the top of this risotto. If you obtain them a few days in advance, put them inside the bag of rice, which will then pick up their flavour before you start cooking. You can flavour eggs with truffles in the same way.

1 Heat a tablespoon of the olive oil in a pan, add half the shallots and half the garlic and cook until just softened. Season and set aside in a large bowl.

2 In a large frying pan, heat another spoonful of the oil and cook each variety of mushroom separately, letting them sear on one side, then turning them over and taking them out when they just colour. Put them in the bowl with the shallots and garlic, season really well and stir in the chopped parsley. Keep warm while you make the risotto.

3 Bring the stock to the boil in a pan, then reduce the heat so it is just simmering.

4 Heat the butter and the remaining olive oil in a large, heavy-based pan. Add the remaining shallots and cook gently until just translucent. Add the remaining garlic and half the dried mushrooms and cook for 3–4 minutes.

5 Meanwhile, crush the rest of the dried mushrooms to a powder in a pestle and mortar and mix with some salt and pepper, then set aside.

6 Add the rice to the pan and stir around for a couple of minutes to coat it with the fat. Raise the heat slightly and add a couple of ladlefuls of the hot stock. Stir around with a spatula until all the liquid has been absorbed.

7 Keep adding the stock a ladleful at a time, stirring and scraping constantly to prevent sticking. After about 15 minutes, test a grain of rice; it should be tender but still firm to the bite and the risotto should be creamy and moist. If it's not quite ready, keep cooking for a few minutes longer, adding small quantities of stock (or boiling water if you have used up all the stock).

8 When the risotto is ready, add the Parmesan cheese and the knob of butter and beat like mad to incorporate them into the risotto, so that you get that wonderful creamy, soft, voluminous texture. Gently stir in the cooked mushroom mixture, followed by the powdered dried mushrooms. Serve immediately.

Desserts

Arabian Nights Figs

Emma says that she is inspired by Nigella Lawson. She loves her uncomplicated food and the flavour that comes from good ingredients used simply. These baked figs go very soggy and are completely moreish. Use as much lemon juice as you want, as it helps to cut through the sweetness. Both the rose and orange-flower waters should be available from good healthfood shops. If you can't find them, you can substitute very fragrant honey.

→ 150G (5OZ) CASTER SUGAR
→ 1 CINNAMON STICK
→ 2 TBSP ROSEWATER
→ 2 TBSP ORANGE-FLOWER WATER
→ JUICE OF 1 LEMON
→ 8 RIPE BUT FIRM FRESH FIGS
→ 150G (5OZ) MASCARPONE CHEESE
→ 2 TSP ICING SUGAR

1 Preheat the oven to 180°C/350°F/Gas Mark 4.

2 Put the caster sugar in a small, heavy-based saucepan with 150ml (¼ pint) water and heat gently, stirring occasionally, until dissolved. Add the cinnamon stick and boil for 5 minutes. Add the rosewater, orange-flower water and lemon juice and bring back to the boil.

3 Cut a deep cross in the top of each fig and fit them snugly into a small baking dish. Spoon the syrup over the top of each fig and bake for about 15 minutes, until tender. Meanwhile, mix the mascarpone and icing sugar together.

4 Remove the figs from the oven, and spoon a little sweetened mascarpone into the centre of each one. Divide between 4 dessert bowls, spooning the syrup around the figs. Serve immediately, with any remaining mascarpone.

'If I were to go home and go to bed with a dessert, I'd be going home and going to bed with this!'
John Torode, Masterchef Judge, to contestant Emma Corbett

Inspired by contestant Sandy Byrne

Aromatic Pears Baked in Dessert Wine

This simple recipe has a real kick to it, due to the amount of booze it contains. Choose the pears carefully. A soft pear will take a lot less time to cook than a hard one. Served either hot or cold, this is delicious with vanilla ice cream.

→ 4 FIRM CONFERENCE OR OTHER DESSERT PEARS
→ 3 TBSP VANILLA-FLAVOURED CASTER SUGAR
→ ABOUT 175ML (6FL OZ) BEAUMES DE VENISE (OR SIMILAR DESSERT WINE)
→ 2 STAR ANISE
→ 1 CINNAMON STICK
→ 200ML (7FL OZ) CRÈME FRAÎCHE

1 Preheat the oven to 200°C/400°F/Gas Mark 6.

2 Peel the pears, cut them lengthways into quarters and remove the core. Place in an ovenproof dish in a single layer. Sprinkle 2 tablespoons of the vanilla sugar over them and pour in enough wine to come about halfway up the pear quarters.

3 Add the star anise. Break the cinnamon stick into 3 or 4 pieces and spread amongst the pears, making sure the spices are submerged so they infuse the liquor and flavour the pears.

4 Bake for 20–25 minutes, until the pears are beginning to caramelise, basting them with the cooking liquor about halfway through. Meanwhile, mix the crème fraîche with the remaining vanilla sugar and chill until ready to serve.

5 Remove the pears from the oven and pour the cooking liquor and spices into a small saucepan. Simmer until reduced by one third and slightly thickened.

6 Divide the pears between 4 serving dishes. Spoon the syrup over them and serve warm, with the crème fraîche.

Baked Honey Peaches with Spiced Yoghurt

This simple treatment really brings out the best in peaches. The rich and perfumed flavour of the stone fruit, with its concentrated sweetness, is complemented by the spiced yoghurt. Nectarines would work equally well.

→ 4 RIPE PEACHES, HALVED AND STONED
→ 50G (2OZ) FLAKED ALMONDS
→ 4 TBSP ORANGE BLOSSOM HONEY
→ 4 TBSP CASTER SUGAR
→ A TINY PINCH OF SAFFRON (4–5 STRANDS)
→ GRATED ZEST AND JUICE OF 1 ORANGE
→ 2 TBSP BRANDY
→ ½ TSP GROUND CINNAMON
→ 150G (5OZ) GREEK-STYLE YOGHURT

1 Preheat the oven to 180°C/350°F/Gas Mark 4.

2 Arrange the peaches cut-side up in an ovenproof dish. Mix the almonds and honey together and place in the cavity of the peach halves. Sprinkle half the sugar on top.

3 Dry-roast the saffron for a few seconds in a small saucepan over a low heat, then stir in the rest of the sugar plus the orange zest and juice. Remove from the heat and leave to infuse for 10 minutes. Stir in the brandy and pour around the peaches.

4 Place in the oven and bake for 20 minutes, until the peaches are tender. Place 2 peach halves on each serving plate and spoon some of the fruit liquor on top. Mix the cinnamon into the yoghurt and serve with the fruit.

'Looking for new ideas, new ingredients, being creative and not producing poncey food! That's what's important.'
Peter Richards, Masterchef Mentor

Inspired by contestant Anna Mosesson

Glazed Apples and Almonds with Amaretto and Clotted Cream

If you covered this apple dish with pastry and then baked it for a good 20 minutes, it would make a fantastic *tarte Tatin*. When cooking with apples, it is important to choose the right variety. Here you need dessert apples, which keep their shape during cooking but become translucent and soft.

→ 3 BRAEBURN APPLES
→ 50G (2OZ) UNSALTED BUTTER
→ 4 TBSP CASTER SUGAR
→ 100ML (3½FL OZ) AMARETTO LIQUEUR
→ 50G (2OZ) FLAKED ALMONDS, TOASTED
→ 1 VANILLA POD
→ 100G (4OZ) CLOTTED CREAM

1 Peel and core the apples, then cut each one into 12 wedges.

2 Melt the butter in a heavy-based saucepan over a moderate heat. Add the apples and sauté until they start to colour.

3 Stir in the sugar and Amaretto. Bring to the boil, then reduce the heat and simmer for about 5 minutes, until the liquid has reduced to a caramel sauce (if it is too thin, remove the apples with a slotted spoon and boil the sauce until reduced and thickened). Stir in the toasted almonds.

4 Slit open the vanilla pod lengthways and scrape the seeds into a small bowl. Add the clotted cream and mix well. Serve the glazed apples and almonds accompanied by the clotted cream.

'I'm looking for the contestants to express their personalities through their food ... What you're saying is "This is me." That's why different chefs have such different styles of cooking.'
Peter Richards, Masterchef Mentor

Inspired by contestant Mark Todd

Caramelised Apple Pancakes with Vanilla Milk Sorbet

These thin, delicate pancakes are used to wrap round the apples and their lovely caramel sauce but in fact the recipe would be just as good with a stack of thick, American-style buttermilk pancakes. Either way, serve steaming hot, with the milk sorbet on top to melt into the apples.

- → 50G (2OZ) UNSALTED BUTTER
- → 3 LARGE PINK LADY APPLES, CORED AND SLICED
- → 4 TBSP CASTER SUGAR
- → 2 TBSP CALVADOS
- → ICING SUGAR FOR DUSTING

For the vanilla milk sorbet:
- → 100G (4OZ) CASTER SUGAR
- → 150ML (1/4 PINT) DOUBLE CREAM
- → 150ML (1/4 PINT) JERSEY GOLD-TOP MILK
- → A FEW DROPS OF VANILLA EXTRACT
- → 2 TSP LIQUID GLYCERINE

For the pancakes:
- → 100G (4OZ) PLAIN FLOUR
- → 2 TSP ICING SUGAR
- → 1 LARGE EGG, LIGHTLY BEATEN
- → 300ML (1/2 PINT) MILK
- → 15G (1/2OZ) BUTTER, MELTED
- → 2 TBSP GROUNDNUT OIL

1 First make the sorbet. Bring the sugar and cream to the boil in a small saucepan, then remove from the heat and stir until the sugar has dissolved. Stir in the milk, vanilla extract and glycerine. Pour the mixture into 4 small ramekin dishes (they should be half full). Place in the freezer for about 1 hour, until just frozen.

2 For the pancakes, sift the flour and icing sugar into a bowl. Whisk in the egg and a little of the milk to make a smooth paste, then whisk in the remaining milk and the melted butter. Continue to whisk until the surface is covered with little bubbles. Pour into a jug and leave to rest for 30 minutes.

3 For the apples, melt the butter in a large frying pan, add the apple slices and fry until tinged with gold and beginning to soften. Stir in the sugar and Calvados and cook until the sugar has dissolved and the apples are tender and lightly caramelised. Remove from the heat and keep warm.

4 To cook the pancakes, heat about a teaspoon of the groundnut oil in a heavy-based 18cm (7 in) frying pan. When it is very hot, swirl it around to ensure it coats the base of the pan, then pour off any excess. Pour in just enough batter to create a thin skin on the base of the pan. Cook over a moderate heat until the pancake is golden brown underneath, then turn and cook the other side until golden. Repeat with the remaining batter, oiling the pan each time. The mixture should make 8–10 pancakes. Stack the pancakes between sheets of baking parchment and keep warm until ready to serve.

5 To serve, remove the sorbet from the freezer and leave at room temperature for a couple of minutes. Divide the apples between the pancakes, roll them up and place on 4 serving plates. Turn out the sorbet on to the plates. Sift a little icing sugar over the pancakes and serve.

Name: Helen Cristofoli
Age: 39
Occupation: I have my own food and drink PR business.
Place of residence: London
Why did you apply to Masterchef?
Because I fancied a new challenge in my life. I love food and I wanted to see how far I could get. Also because I had no idea how scary it would be!
What do you cook at home and who do you cook for?
I live alone, but I cook for friends and family and have lots of dinner parties. I cook everything from Italian and Chinese to Thai and more. I'm very adventurous. I'll try everything. Instead of Turkey for Christmas last year I devised lots of dishes all based around fish; then I cooked home-made spring rolls, duck with pancakes, lemon chicken, and loads of different recipes from scratch for Chinese New Year too. And for my therapy, I bake cakes when I want to relax.
What is your favourite meal?
Chocolate, chocolate and more chocolate! But if I had to make a meal it would be a risotto, because it's Italian and I'm Italian. It's cosy and homely.
What are your aspirations in the world of cooking and food?
The Masterchef experience gave me the confidence to leave the job I was doing and set up by myself. As long as I'm happy doing what I'm doing with food and drink and learning, I am happy, but I would love to eventually present or write about food and drink. And invent a low-calorie chocolate cake!

Name: James Cross
Age: 24
Occupation: I'm an organic vegetable farmer, but I'm also a year away from qualifying as a barrister.
Place of residence: Birmingham
Why did you apply to Masterchef?
It was chance really: I was talking to a member of my family, they'd seen the form in a magazine and I filled it out not really expecting anything to come of it. I never really had a desire to be a TV cook. I was very excited to get a phone call from a researcher and then started to take it all more seriously.
What do you cook at home and who do you cook for?
I cook for my girlfriend, friends and family. I cook anything that's seasonal. Seasonality is my thing – I'd rather do without asparagus in November and wait until it's ready to pick from the ground in April.
What is your favourite meal?
My favourite time of year for eating is mid-autumn, I love it when wild mushrooms come out. I pick them and sell chanterelles and trompettes to restaurants and cook with them at home. I've picked 17 of the top variety for eating, and that's on the outskirts of Birmingham! I'd love to find a truffle.
What are your aspirations in the world of cooking and food?
My aspiration in the world of cooking is to eat well. My long-term goal would be to supply really good-quality ingredients and delicacies from around the world to the best restaurants.

Name: Simon Cathcart
Age: 34
Occupation: I work as a purchasing consultant to the hospitality industry.
Place of residence: South of Glasgow
Why did you apply to Masterchef?
I saw the advert online and sent in an application straight away. I knew it was something I wanted to do. I love cooking, going on national TV appealed to me and I'm a real foodie!
What do you cook at home and who do you cook for?
I do all of the cooking at home – for dinner parties, for my wife and my kids. I love to get the kids involved in cooking, to try things they haven't had before, to learn what's good and bad for you. I find cooking really therapeutic, so quite often I just cook for myself. You don't have to be overly fancy for things to taste good, but I do spend a long time making sure things are well presented. I aspire to Michelin star level!
What is your favourite meal?
I love cooking with fish and seafood especially. There is so much variety in the textures and flavours in seafood and there are so many ways of cooking it.
What are your aspirations in the world of cooking and food?
Ultimately I want to own my own restaurant. I've always had a hankering to have my own restaurant ever since I was the only boy in my Home Economics class at school. I want to use my own ideas, innovation and cooking skills.

Ginger Upside-down Cakes with Ginger Crème Fraîche and Caramelised Figs

These little puddings are quintessential comfort food. A good helping of custard would not be out of place. The ginger syrup is one of those useful baking ingredients that can change an otherwise plain pudding into something both flavourful and moist, as it helps to stabilise the mixture.

→ 75G (3OZ) UNSALTED BUTTER, PLUS A SMALL KNOB OF BUTTER FOR GREASING
→ 75G (3OZ) CASTER SUGAR, PLUS A LITTLE EXTRA FOR DUSTING
→ 3–4 PIECES OF STEM GINGER IN SYRUP, SLICED INTO THIN ROUNDS
→ 4 TSP SYRUP FROM THE STEM GINGER JAR
→ 1 EGG, LIGHTLY BEATEN
→ GRATED ZEST OF 1 LEMON
→ 75G (3OZ) SELF-RAISING FLOUR

For the caramelised figs:
→ 4 FRESH FIGS, QUARTERED
→ 200G (7OZ) CASTER SUGAR

For the ginger crème fraîche:
→ 200G (7OZ) CRÈME FRAÎCHE
→ 3 TBSP SYRUP FROM THE STEM GINGER JAR

MASTERCHEF TOP TIP

When you are buying figs, to find really ripe ones pick them up gently and look underneath. If there are little droplets that look like leaking sap, take them home and eat them immediately – they're beautifully ripe!
John Torode, Masterchef Judge

1 Preheat the oven to 180°C/350°F/Gas Mark 4.

2 Grease 4 ramekin dishes with the knob of butter and dust them with a little caster sugar. Line the base of each dish with the ginger slices and spoon a teaspoon of the ginger syrup on top.

3 Cream the butter and caster sugar together until light and fluffy. Gradually add the egg, beating well after each addition, then stir in the lemon zest. Sift in the flour and gently fold it in, using a large metal spoon. Divide the mixture between the ramekins and level the surface. Put the ramekins in a roasting tin containing enough hot water to come halfway up the sides of the dishes. Bake for 30 minutes, until risen and golden.

4 Meanwhile, put the quartered figs on to a baking tray lined with baking parchment. Gently heat the caster sugar in a medium heavy-based saucepan until it melts. Raise the heat and cook, without stirring, until it turns a light golden brown. Immediately pour this caramel over the fig quarters and leave to cool.

5 When the puddings are done, remove them from the oven and leave to cool for a few minutes, then turn them out on to individual plates.

6 Mix the crème fraîche and stem ginger syrup in a bowl. Place the caramelised figs and 2 tablespoons of ginger crème fraîche on each plate with the ginger upside-down cake. Serve warm.

'I adored that pud – I could have eaten a bucketful!'
Gregg Wallace, Masterchef Judge

Mango and Ginger Flapjack Crumble

Katherine continued to thrill all through her journey. This flapjack crumble makes a perfect family dessert, with just the right combination of crisp topping and soft fruit.

→ 1 RIPE MANGO, PEELED, STONED
AND FINELY DICED
→ 1 PIECE OF STEM GINGER IN SYRUP,
FINELY CHOPPED
→ 25G (1OZ) BUTTER
→ 1 TBSP DEMERARA SUGAR
→ 2 TBSP GOLDEN SYRUP
→ 75G (3OZ) PORRIDGE OATS
→ ½ TSP GROUND GINGER
→ 4 TBSP GREEK YOGHURT

1 Preheat the oven to 160°C/325°F/Gas Mark 3.

2 Mix the mango and stem ginger together and divide between 4 ramekin dishes.

3 Put the butter, sugar and syrup in a small saucepan and heat gently until melted. Remove from the heat and stir in the oats and ground ginger. Spoon this mixture over the fruit.

4 Bake for about 30 minutes, until the topping is golden. Serve with the Greek yoghurt.

'The only purple food should be in science fiction movies!'
Gregg Wallace, Masterchef Judge, to a contestant

Inspired by contestant Milla Mackey

Panettone Bread and Butter Pudding with Whisky Sauce

Panettone makes a luxurious bread and butter pudding, transforming a simple dessert into something very special indeed. The story behind it goes something like this: a poor apprentice baker found that he had no money to buy his sweetheart a Christmas present, so after he finished work on Christmas Eve he asked his boss if he could make a special present for his loved one. He baked the most beautiful light fruitcake, rich in vanilla, butter and candied peel. She, of course, was smitten.

→ 350ML (12FL OZ) MILK
→ 150ML (¼ PINT) SINGLE CREAM
→ 3 TBSP COARSE-CUT SEVILLE ORANGE MARMALADE
→ 4 EGGS
→ 200G (7OZ) PANETTONE, SLICED
→ 40G (1½OZ) UNSALTED BUTTER
→ FRESHLY GRATED NUTMEG
→ 25G (1OZ) DEMERARA SUGAR

For the whisky sauce:
→ 200G (7OZ) MASCARPONE CHEESE
→ 1 TBSP WHISKY LIQUEUR (GLAYVA OR SIMILAR)
→ 1 TBSP ICING SUGAR, SIFTED

1 Preheat the oven to 180°C/350°F/Gas Mark 4.

2 Pour the milk and cream into a saucepan and heat gently to simmering point, but do not let them boil. Add half the marmalade and stir until melted.

3 Lightly whisk the eggs together in a large bowl and pour the hot milk on to them, stirring all the time. Strain through a sieve.

4 Spread the panettone with the butter and cut it into triangles. Arrange in a buttered ovenproof dish about 23 x 18cm (9 x 7 in). Pour the egg mixture over the panettone, then finely grate a little nutmeg over and sprinkle the demerara sugar on top. Leave to stand for 10 minutes to allow the liquid to soak in.

5 Bake the pudding for 20–25 minutes, until just set and lightly browned. Meanwhile, mix all the ingredients for the whisky sauce together in a bowl.

6 Remove the pudding from the oven and brush the top with the remaining marmalade. Return to the oven for a few minutes to glaze. Serve the pudding warm, accompanied by the whisky sauce.

Inspired by contestant Christopher Souto

Individual Brioche Puddings with Caramel Sauce

This wonderful little pudding by Christopher is truly the best type of comfort food. Although it sounds similar to bread and butter pudding, the centre is more unctuous and creamy, while the outer casing of brioche becomes lovely and crisp. The caramel sauce can be used for pouring over vanilla ice cream as well as profiteroles or a classic sponge pudding.

- → A SMALL KNOB OF BUTTER FOR GREASING
- → 2 TBSP CASTER SUGAR, PLUS A LITTLE EXTRA FOR DUSTING
- → 200G (7OZ) BRIOCHE, CRUSTS REMOVED
- → 200ML (7FL OZ) WHOLE MILK
- → 300ML (½ PINT) SINGLE CREAM
- → 3 EGG YOLKS
- → 1 HEAPED TSP CORNFLOUR
- → 150G (5OZ) RAISINS
- → 1½ TSP GROUND CINNAMON

For the caramel sauce:
- → 100G (4OZ) LIGHT SOFT BROWN SUGAR
- → 50G (2OZ) UNSALTED BUTTER
- → 150ML (¼ PINT) DOUBLE CREAM

1 Preheat the oven to 180°C/350°F/Gas Mark 4. Butter 4 individual pudding bowls or ramekin dishes, about 200ml (7fl oz) in capacity, and dust them with a little caster sugar.

2 Cut the brioche into 12 thin slices and toast lightly on one side. Cut out 4 circles and use to line the base of the dishes, toasted-side down. Cut the rest of the brioche into fat 'fingers', reserving any trimmings. Use the fingers of brioche to line the sides of the dishes, toasted-side outwards. Make sure they fit snugly, with no gaps.

3 Bring the milk and single cream to boiling point in a saucepan, then cool slightly. Beat the egg yolks, cornflour and sugar together in a bowl. Slowly whisk the hot, creamy milk into the egg mixture, then strain it into a clean saucepan. Cook the custard over a low heat, stirring constantly, until it begins to thicken. Do not let it boil.

4 Remove the custard from the heat and stir in the raisins, cinnamon and brioche trimmings. The mixture should be quite sloppy. Leave to stand for 5 minutes, then spoon the mixture into the lined dishes, filling them to just below the top. Leave to stand for 10 minutes.

5 Place the dishes on a baking tray and bake for 10–15 minutes, until just set.

6 Meanwhile, make the sauce. Put all the ingredients in a heavy-based saucepan and cook over a gentle heat until the mixture is smooth and has thickened to a creamy consistency.

7 Turn the puddings out on to individual plates and pour a little caramel sauce over the top. Serve immediately.

Bakewell Tart with Quince Jam and Nibbed Almonds

Regardless of what is new and trendy, classics such as this Bakewell tart are always fantastic. Thomasina used her own quince jam but you could use any type of jam or jelly.

→ 4 TBSP QUINCE JAM
→ 40G (1½OZ) UNSALTED BUTTER, SOFTENED
→ 50G (2OZ) CASTER SUGAR
→ 1 LARGE EGG, LIGHTLY WHISKED
→ GRATED ZEST OF ½ LEMON
→ 50G (2OZ) GROUND ALMONDS
→ 40G (1½OZ) BLANCHED ALMONDS, ROUGHLY CHOPPED
→ ICING SUGAR FOR DUSTING
→ 150ML (¼ PINT) DOUBLE CREAM, TO SERVE

For the pastry:
→ 100G (4OZ) PLAIN FLOUR
→ 65G (2½OZ) UNSALTED BUTTER
→ 25G (1OZ) ICING SUGAR, SIFTED
→ 1 LARGE EGG YOLK

For the quince syrup:
→ 3 TBSP QUINCE JAM
→ 3 TBSP SAUTERNES OR OTHER SWEET WHITE WINE

1 To make the pastry, sift the flour into a bowl and rub in the butter until the mixture resembles fine breadcrumbs. Stir in the icing sugar, followed by the egg yolk and mix to a firm dough. Cover with cling film and chill for 30 minutes.

2 Roll out the pastry on a lightly floured surface and use to line a lightly greased 18cm (7 in) flan tin. Chill for 10 minutes.

3 Preheat the oven to 180°C/350°F/Gas Mark 4. Gently melt the quince jam in a small pan and spread it over the base of the pastry case. Return the pastry case to the fridge.

4 Beat the butter and caster sugar together in a bowl until light and fluffy. Beat in the egg, lemon zest and ground almonds, then stir in the blanched almonds.

5 Pour this mixture into the pastry case and bake for about 25 minutes, until it turns a light golden brown. The filling should be just set and not too firm. Remove the tart from the oven and leave to rest for 5 minutes, then transfer to a wire rack and leave to cool completely. Dust with icing sugar.

6 Put the quince jam and Sauternes in a small saucepan and stir over a low heat until the jam has melted to form a syrup. Serve the Bakewell tart at room temperature, with the quince syrup and double cream.

Masterchef Masterclass
John Torode's Pastry

Making pastry is a fantastic skill to master. It isn't difficult and it opens the way to so many different dishes, from robust savoury pies and pasties to refined quiches and the entire range of sweet tarts. Very few pastry products that you buy in the shops can equal a home-made tart or pie straight from the oven.

Whatever type of pastry you are making, the aim is a crisp, light result. This is achieved by using soft flour (i.e. ordinary plain white flour), which is low in gluten, and a high proportion of fat to give a characteristic 'short' texture. Butter gives the best flavour and colour, although some savoury pastries include lard for a flaky texture. A little liquid, usually water or egg, binds the dough. If you use egg, it also enriches it and makes it more pliable.

Pastry should be mixed quickly and lightly so the gluten in the flour doesn't develop too much, otherwise the dough will be stretchy and more likely to shrink during cooking. You don't need a marble worktop: although it is correct that the ingredients, especially for sweet and shortcrust pastry, should be cool, the most important thing is to get the proportions right – no amount of cooling will help if you put too much butter in the mixture

Many people are nervous about trying pastry recipes, but there are a few steps that you can follow to take the pressure off and allow you to relax and be confident of success:

→ Be gentle with pastry and the results will be perfect.
→ Get to know your oven and its peculiarities – particularly if you use a fan oven, where you may have to adjust the temperature.
→ Keep your work surface and tart tins spotlessly clean.
→ Keep all your ingredients cool, including the flour.
→ Cold hands are important, too. If you have warm hands, run them under the cold tap for a minute or so and dry them well before you start making pastry.
→ Tough pastry comes from being worked too much, so mix it quickly and lightly and roll it out only once.
→ Use a cool, well-floured work surface for rolling out.
→ Grease the tin with the smallest possible amount of butter.
→ Pre-bake the pastry before adding the filling (this is known as baking blind), for a crisp outer shell without a soggy bottom.

John Torode's
Sweet Shortcrust Pastry

- → 150G (5OZ) UNSALTED BUTTER
- → 300G (10OZ) PLAIN WHITE FLOUR
- → 100G (4OZ) CASTER SUGAR
- → GRATED ZEST OF 1 LEMON
- → 2 MEDIUM EGGS

This is based on the traditional French pâte sucrée, with a high proportion of sugar and egg for a rich, biscuity texture. It is the base for all those great classic sweet tarts, from a sharp, tangy lemon tart to the perfect chocolate tart.

1 Dice the butter and leave it to soften at room temperature for 30 minutes.

2 Sift the flour into a large bowl, make a well in the centre and add the butter and sugar. Work in the butter with your fingertips until the mixture resembles fine breadcrumbs. Stir in the lemon zest.

3 Break in the eggs and, using your fingertips, bring everything together. Turn out on to a floured work surface and knead lightly by pushing the dough away with the heel of your hand 3 times, giving it a quarter turn each time. You should end up with a silky-smooth ball of dough.

4 Wrap the pastry in cling film and leave it to rest in the fridge for about an hour before using (it will keep in the fridge for 3–4 days at this stage and also freezes well).

5 Unwrap the pastry and place it on a lightly floured work surface. Gently push down on the pastry with a rolling pin, then give it a quarter turn and repeat. Do this 4 times, so the pastry begins to flatten out.

6 Start to roll out the pastry, moving it around on the work surface from time to time to prevent sticking; if necessary, dust the work surface and the rolling pin with more flour. Roll out to about 5mm ($^1/_4$ in) thick (if you become nervous about it tearing, you can always stop before it gets this thin).

7 Lift the pastry up on the rolling pin and lay it over a lightly greased 25cm (10 in) loose-bottomed fluted tart tin. Ease the pastry down the sides to fit the tin, being careful to push it right down into the corners and making sure there are no

gaps between the pastry and the tin. Instead of using warm fingers, which may melt the pastry, you could make a small ball of excess dough and use it to press the pastry gently into the tin. Lightly run the rolling pin over the top of the tin to remove excess pastry, then push the pastry up slightly all the way round, if possible, so it is a little higher than the side of the tin. Chill for about 10 minutes.

8 To bake blind, preheat the oven to 200°C/400°F/Gas Mark 6 and place a baking sheet in it. Line the pastry case with a sheet of baking parchment, bringing it right up the sides. Fill with dried beans or rice, then place in the oven on the hot baking sheet and bake for 15 minutes, until the base of the pastry case is pale and chalky looking.

9 Remove the paper and filling (the beans or rice can be reused whenever you make pastry) and reduce the oven temperature to 150°C/300°F/Gas Mark 2. Return the pastry case to the oven for 15 minutes, until the base is a uniform pale-golden brown. Leave to cool.

John Torode's
Shortcrust Pastry

→ 300G (11OZ) PLAIN WHITE FLOUR
→ 150G (5OZ) UNSALTED BUTTER, CUT INTO SMALL PIECES
→ 1 MEDIUM EGG YOLK
→ 4 TBSP ICED WATER

This is not as rich as Sweet Shortcrust Pastry. It is suitable for all savoury tarts and pies, and can also be used for desserts such as apple pie or treacle tart.

1 Put the flour and butter in a mixing bowl and, using a knife or your fingertips, work them together until they look like fine breadcrumbs (alternatively, do this in a food processor, using the pulse button).

2 Add the egg yolk and water. Bring everything together into a ball, but don't knead. Wrap in cling film and leave to rest in the fridge for at least an hour (it will keep in the fridge for 3–4 days at this stage and also freezes well).

3 Roll out the pastry and use to line a lightly greased 25cm (10 in) loose-bottomed tart tin, following the instructions in steps 6 and 7 for Sweet Shortcrust Pastry (see pages 168–9).

4 Bake the pastry case blind as for Sweet Shortcrust Pastry (see pages 168–9), but leave it in the oven for 20 minutes before removing the paper and beans or rice. Then bake for a further 5 minutes, still at 200°C/400°F/Gas Mark 6, until the pastry is pale golden. Leave to cool.

John Torode's
Passion Fruit Tart

SERVES 8–10

→ 1 QUANTITY OF SWEET
   SHORTCRUST PASTRY (SEE PAGE 168)
→ 175ML (6FL OZ) PASSION FRUIT PULP
   (AVAILABLE IN CANS)
→ 200G (7OZ) CASTER SUGAR
→ 5 EGGS
→ 200ML (7FL OZ) DOUBLE CREAM
→ 150ML (¼ PINT) WHIPPING CREAM,
   LIGHTLY WHIPPED
→ SEEDS AND PULP FROM 3 RIPE
   PASSION FRUIT

This recipe has never let me down. Follow it carefully and you will not be disappointed.

1 Roll out the pastry and use it to line a 25cm (10 in) tart tin. Bake it blind as described on pages 168–9. Remove from the oven and place on a baking sheet. Raise the oven temperature to 180°C/350°F/Gas Mark 4.

2 Whisk the passion fruit pulp and sugar together. In a separate bowl, whisk the eggs together, then whisk in the double cream until well combined. Gently whisk this mixture into the sweetened fruit pulp, then pass through a fine sieve and pour this custard into the pastry case.

3 Place in the oven and bake for 35–40 minutes. Press the surface gently with your finger to check if it is set, returning it to the oven for another 5 minutes if it is still too liquid. It should wobble slightly, like a set jelly.

4 Leave the tart to cool to room temperature, then serve each portion with a spoonful of whipped cream garnished with the fresh passion fruit.

Lemon and Plum Tart with Crème Fraîche

This tart relies upon frangipane, an almond and butter paste, to give it body and form. If you can't get plums, then apricots or nectarines would work just as well.

- → 75G (3OZ) UNSALTED BUTTER, SOFTENED
- → 100G (4OZ) CASTER SUGAR
- → 2 LARGE EGGS, LIGHTLY BEATEN
- → GRATED ZEST OF 1 LEMON
- → 100G (4OZ) GROUND ALMONDS
- → 3 PLUMS, HALVED, STONED AND CUT INTO 6 WEDGES EACH
- → 4 TBSP MELTED BUTTER
- → 1 TSP ICING SUGAR
- → 150ML (¼ PINT) CRÈME FRAÎCHE

For the pastry:
- → 200G (7OZ) PLAIN FLOUR
- → 90G (3OZ) UNSALTED BUTTER
- → 40G (1½OZ) CASTER SUGAR
- → 1 MEDIUM EGG, LIGHTLY BEATEN

1 First make the pastry. Sift the flour into a bowl and rub in the butter with your fingertips until the mixture resembles fine breadcrumbs. Stir in the sugar. Add the egg and mix to a firm dough. Cover with cling film and chill for 30 minutes.

2 Roll out the pastry on a floured surface and use to line a lightly greased deep 18cm (7 in) flan tin. Chill for 10 minutes.

3 Preheat the oven to 180°C/350°F/Gas Mark 4. For the filling, cream the butter and caster sugar together in a bowl until light and fluffy. Beat in the eggs, a little at a time, followed by the lemon zest and ground almonds.

4 Pour this almond cream into the pastry case and arrange the plums on top, overlapping them slightly. Brush with the melted butter and sift the icing sugar over the fruit.

5 Bake for 20–25 minutes, until the almond cream swells up around the fruit and turns a light golden brown. Remove the tart from the oven and leave to rest for 5 minutes. Transfer to a wire rack and leave to cool. Serve at room temperature, accompanied by the crème fraîche.

Fig Tarts with Crème de Cassis Ice Cream

What a shame that no one got to taste these little tarts at Masterchef: as they were being taken from the bench to be finished in the oven, they fell on to the floor! However, the cassis ice cream was very good. We all have little disasters in the kitchen – it's part of the learning process. Unfortunately for Scott, that learning process was on national television. Tough!

→ 225G (8OZ) PUFF PASTRY
→ 4 TBSP MASCARPONE CHEESE
→ 4 LARGE, FRESH FIGS
→ 4 TSP MUSCOVADO SUGAR
→ 2 TSP RUNNY HONEY
  For the ice cream:
→ 100G (4OZ) CASTER SUGAR
→ 340G (12OZ) PLAIN YOGHURT
→ 100ML (3½FL OZ) CRÈME FRAÎCHE
→ 5 TBSP CRÈME DE CASSIS

1 For the cassis ice cream, mix all the ingredients together and place in an ice-cream maker. Churn for 25–30 minutes, until the mixture has thickened but is not completely frozen. Pour into a container and freeze to finish.

2 For the tarts, preheat the oven to 230°C/450°F/Gas Mark 8. Roll the puff pastry out thinly and cut out four 12cm (5 in) circles. Place them on a baking sheet brushed with a little cold water. Use a sharp knife to draw a 1cm (½ in) rim around the edges. Lightly prick the area inside the rim with a fork. Chill for 30 minutes.

3 Spoon the mascarpone into the middle of each pastry circle, leaving the rim clear. Cut each fig into 6 and arrange on top of the mascarpone in a fan shape. Sprinkle with the sugar and drizzle the honey over the fruit.

4 Bake for 8–10 minutes, until well coloured. Serve warm, with the ice cream.

'You've got everything in there ... if you could have got hold of a tube of Smarties, they'd have gone in there as well.'
Gregg Wallace, Masterchef Judge, to a contestant

Inspired by contestant Xanthe Milton

Chocolate Brownies and Ice Cream

There is little better in life than ice cream and chocolate. When that chocolate comes in the form of a brownie, then it becomes a real treat! Use a good-quality chocolate for the brownies in this recipe. Xanthe used Green & Black's organic chocolate but any chocolate containing about 70 per cent cocoa solids will work just as well.

→ 250G (9OZ) BUTTER, SOFTENED
→ 250G (9OZ) GOOD-QUALITY DARK CHOCOLATE, BROKEN INTO PIECES
→ 250G (9OZ) SOFT DARK BROWN SUGAR
→ 250G (9OZ) SELF-RAISING FLOUR
→ 4 EGG YOLKS, LIGHTLY BEATEN
→ 4-6 TBSP MILK

For the ice cream:
→ 300ML (½ PINT) DOUBLE CREAM
→ 300ML (½ PINT) MILK
→ 1 VANILLA POD
→ 6 EGG YOLKS
→ 175G (6OZ) CASTER SUGAR
→ 2 TBSP FINELY GRATED LEMON ZEST

1 First make the brownies. Preheat the oven to 150°C/300°F/ Gas Mark 2. Lightly grease a 30 x 23cm (12 x 9in) baking tray.

2 Melt the butter and chocolate in a bowl set over a pan of simmering water. Remove from the heat and stir in the sugar, then leave to cool slightly.

3 Sift the flour into a large bowl, make a well in the centre and pour in the chocolate mixture. Gradually stir the flour into the mixture until well blended. Beat in the eggs, then stir in enough milk to give a soft dropping consistency. Spoon the mixture into the prepared tray.

4 Bake for 25–30 minutes, until just set. Leave to cool before cutting into squares.

5 For the ice cream, pour the cream and milk into a saucepan, then slit the vanilla pod open lengthways and scrape the seeds into the pan. Bring slowly to the boil.

6 Meanwhile, whisk the egg yolks and sugar together in a bowl until pale and light. Pour in the hot cream and stir until well blended. Pour into a clean saucepan and cook over a very low heat, stirring constantly, until the custard has thickened enough to coat the back of the spoon. Strain through a sieve into a bowl and leave to cool, stirring occasionally to prevent a skin forming. Stir in the lemon zest.

7 Pour the custard into an ice-cream maker and churn for 20 minutes or until it has thickened and increased in volume but not frozen completely. Pour into a container and finish in the freezer. Serve the chocolate brownies with a good scoop of the ice cream.

Chocolate Fondant with Vanilla Cream

The dessert that launched a thousand smiles. A fondant is simply a chocolate pudding with a melting, gooey centre. Served with cream or ice cream, it really can't be beaten. The correct timing is essential to ensure the centre remains runny, but if you do overcook it, it will still be a good chocolate pudding.

→ 75G (3OZ) UNSALTED BUTTER, PLUS
   A SMALL KNOB OF BUTTER FOR GREASING
→ COCOA POWDER FOR DUSTING
→ 75G (3OZ) GOOD-QUALITY PLAIN CHOCOLATE
   (AT LEAST 70 PER CENT COCOA SOLIDS)
→ 2 LARGE EGGS
→ 1 LARGE EGG YOLK
→ 50G (2OZ) CASTER SUGAR
→ 50G (2OZ) PLAIN FLOUR
→ ICING SUGAR FOR DUSTING
For the vanilla cream:
→ 5 TBSP DOUBLE CREAM
→ 1 TBSP ICING SUGAR, SIFTED
→ ½ VANILLA POD

1 Preheat the oven to 180°C/350°F/Gas Mark 4. Grease 4 ramekins with the knob of butter and dust lightly with cocoa powder.

2 For the vanilla cream, put the double cream and icing sugar into a bowl. Slit the vanilla pod open lengthways and scrape the seeds into the bowl. Whip the cream until it stands in soft peaks, then chill.

3 Put the chocolate and butter in a bowl placed over a pan of simmering water, making sure the water does not touch the base of the bowl. Leave until melted, then stir together.

4 Using a hand-held electric beater, whisk the eggs, egg yolk and sugar together in a large bowl for 6–8 minutes, until thick and creamy. Pour the melted chocolate over the egg mixture and sift in the flour. Carefully fold everything together with a large metal spoon. Pour the mixture into the ramekins, leaving 1cm (½ in) at the top to allow it to rise. Place in the oven and bake for 9–10 minutes, until the fondants are risen round the edges but soft in the centre.

5 Remove the fondants from the oven and turn out on to individual serving plates. Dust with a little icing sugar and serve with the vanilla cream.

Cardamom-flavoured Oranges with Vanilla Minted Cream and Almond Biscuits

With its fashionable North African influences, this beautifully simple dessert will delight anyone who eats it. In fact, it almost made Gregg cry! It is said that the spread of the orange was brought about many centuries ago by the spread of Islam. As the Arabs moved from place to place, they removed all the vines that were used for wine and replaced them with orange trees.

→ 4 ORANGES
→ 2 TBSP CASTER SUGAR
→ 4 GREEN CARDAMOM PODS
→ 25G (1OZ) UNSALTED BUTTER
For the biscuits:
→ 50G (2OZ) PLAIN FLOUR
→ 25G (1OZ) GROUND ALMONDS
→ 15G (½OZ) GOLDEN CASTER SUGAR
→ 25G (1OZ) BUTTER, DICED
→ 1 TBSP ICING SUGAR
For the vanilla minted cream:
→ 150ML (¼ PINT) DOUBLE CREAM
→ 1 TSP NEILSEN-MASSEY PURE VANILLA BEAN PASTE, OR THE SEEDS FROM 1 VANILLA POD
→ 1 TSP ICING SUGAR, SIFTED
→ 2 SPRIGS OF MINT, FINELY CHOPPED

MASTERCHEF TOP TIP
This dessert is simply sublime, and it did indeed almost move me to tears. The combination of a light cream, almond biscuits and a delicate orange flavour is a joy. The oranges must be sweet, without too much acidity. Mandarins or satsumas would work beautifully. To guarantee sweetness, look out for scarring – something that we in the UK avoid like the plague. The fruit that grows on the outside of the tree brushes the leaves while forming, and this produces scars. Only the fruit on the outside of the tree will touch the leaves. And it is the fruit on the outside that gets the most sunshine. Obvious, isn't it, when someone points it out?
Gregg Wallace, Masterchef Judge

1 Preheat the oven to 160°C/325°F/Gas Mark 3.

2 For the biscuits, sift the flour into a mixing bowl and add the ground almonds and caster sugar. Work in the butter with your fingertips, then knead well to make a dough.

3 Shape the mixture into 8 small balls, about the size of a walnut, place on a greased baking sheet and flatten with your fingertips. Bake for about 15 minutes, until lightly coloured around the edges. Remove from the oven and leave to cool. Dust with the icing sugar.

4 Peel the oranges with a sharp knife, cutting away all the white pith. Over a bowl to catch the juice, cut away the orange segments from between the membranes, turning back the flaps of membrane as you go (like turning the pages of a book). When you have finished, squeeze out the juice from the membrane into the bowl. Measure the juice and make it up to 150ml (¼ pint) with water, if necessary.

5 Put the orange juice in a saucepan with the caster sugar, cardamom pods and butter and bring to the boil. Simmer until reduced by half, then remove from the heat and add the orange segments and any juice. Stir the oranges to coat them evenly in the mixture. Remove the cardamom pods and discard.

6 In a separate bowl, whip the cream, vanilla paste or seeds and icing sugar together until they form soft peaks. Fold in the chopped mint. Serve the warm cardamom oranges and syrup with the biscuits and a heaped tablespoon of the cream.

Blackberry Shortcakes with Blackberry and Orange Compote

This is one of the Masterchef crew's favourites, not because it is the work of a culinary genius but because it is the greatest comfort food ever made. It's a simple, scone-like affair served with fresh blackberries and an orange-flavoured blackberry compote. You can make the shortcakes large or small, but smaller ones are prettier.

→ 250G (9OZ) BLACKBERRIES
→ 1½ TBSP CASTER SUGAR
→ GRATED ZEST AND JUICE OF 1 ORANGE
→ 150ML (¼ PINT) DOUBLE CREAM

For the shortcakes:
→ 175G (6OZ) PLAIN FLOUR
→ A PINCH OF SALT
→ 1½ TSP BAKING POWDER
→ 75G (3OZ) UNSALTED BUTTER, FINELY DICED
→ 1½ TBSP CASTER SUGAR, PLUS A LITTLE EXTRA FOR SPRINKLING
→ 1 SMALL EGG
→ 1 TBSP SINGLE CREAM
→ 1 EGG WHITE, LIGHTLY BEATEN

MASTERCHEF TOP TIP

Shortcake is a delightful dessert, not to be confused with shortbread – it's actually more like a scone. Be careful not to overwork the dough, as this will make the cake tough and cause it to shrink as it cooks. A light, aerated mixture is most important.

When cooking the compote, try to keep the definition of the fruit, as this looks more attractive.

Peter Richards, Masterchef Mentor

1 Preheat the oven to 180°C/350°F/Gas Mark 4.

2 To make the shortcakes, sift the flour, salt and baking powder into a large bowl and add the butter and sugar. Rub in the butter until the mixture resembles fine breadcrumbs. Whisk the egg and single cream together and stir into the flour mixture to form a dough. Cover and chill for 30 minutes.

3 On a lightly floured work surface, roll out the dough to 2cm (¾ in) thick. Cut out 4 rounds using a 6.5cm (2 ½ in) cutter. Place on a greased baking sheet, brush with the egg white and sprinkle with a little sugar. Bake for 10–15 minutes, until light golden brown, then leave to cool.

4 For the compote, put half the blackberries in a saucepan with the sugar, orange zest and juice. Cover and cook gently for a few minutes, until the fruit is tender but still holds its shape. Leave to cool.

5 Whip the double cream until it forms soft peaks. Split the shortcakes in half and fill with the cream and fresh blackberries. Drizzle the compote around the shortcakes and serve.

'[That] pud was simple: a perfect understanding of ingredients and how they work.'
Gregg Wallace, Masterchef Judge

Cranachan with Raspberry Tuiles

Cranachan is a classic that's eaten all over Scotland, where it was originally served as a celebration of 'harvest home'.

The quality of the raspberries is crucial to the success of this dish. If they are not ripe and sweet, the whisky and oatmeal cream will overpower, rather than complement them. It is said that Scottish raspberries are the best in the world, so look out for them in late summer and early autumn.

→ 50G (2OZ) PINHEAD OATMEAL
→ 300ML (½ PINT) DOUBLE CREAM
→ 2 TSP CASTER SUGAR
→ 2–3 TBSP DRAMBUIE OR GLAYVA
→ 1 TBSP RUNNY HONEY
→ 1 PUNNET OF FRESH RASPBERRIES
→ ICING SUGAR FOR DUSTING
For the tuiles:
→ 2 EGG WHITES
→ 75G (3OZ) ICING SUGAR
→ 50G (2OZ) PLAIN FLOUR, SIFTED
→ 50G (2OZ) UNSALTED BUTTER, MELTED

MASTERCHEF TOP TIP

To make all the tuile biscuits exactly the same size, trim the edges off a plastic ice-cream lid to create a flat piece of plastic, then draw the size and shape of tuile required on it. Cut the shape out and lay the remaining plastic on the baking sheet. Use a spatula to fill the cut-out area with the biscuit mix, then run the spatula over the top to remove any excess.

John Torode, Masterchef Judge

1 Preheat the oven to 180°C/350°F/Gas Mark 4.

2 For the tuiles, put the egg whites in a bowl, sift in the icing sugar and whisk for 10–15 seconds. Sift in the flour, gently pour in the melted butter and mix to a smooth paste.

3 On a baking tray lined with baking parchment, spread the mixture out into four 10–12cm (4–4½ in) discs with the back of a spoon, leaving space between them so they can spread (any leftover mixture will keep in the fridge for a week).

4 Bake for 8–10 minutes, until the tuiles are golden brown and beginning to bubble. Remove from the oven and drape each one over a lightly greased small, upturned cup or ramekin while still warm. Once cool and crisp, remove from the cup (they will stay crisp for up to 48 hours in an airtight container).

5 Spread the oatmeal out on a baking sheet and toast in the oven for 8–10 minutes, until golden brown. Leave to cool.

6 Whip the double cream, caster sugar, Drambuie and honey together until the mixture just holds its shape. Fold in the toasted oatmeal and then chill.

7 To serve, put a few raspberries into each tuile and top with the cranachan. Decorate with the remaining raspberries and dust with icing sugar. Serve immediately.

Inspired by contestant Helen Cristofoli

Tangerine Soufflé

Some people are intimidated by the thought of making a soufflé but there is no need to be. A soufflé is simply a baked dessert that uses lots of egg white to make it rise. Once you have whipped your egg whites properly, there are two things needed to stop a soufflé collapsing – a steady cooking temperature and a non-convection oven, otherwise the vibrations of the oven can destabilise the mixture and cause the top to fall off. Lastly, make sure that there is a good amount of flavouring, or the soufflé will taste too eggy.

→ A KNOB OF BUTTER FOR GREASING
→ 2 TBSP CASTER SUGAR,
   PLUS EXTRA FOR DUSTING
→ 1 TBSP TANGERINE MARMALADE
→ 2 TBSP FRESH TANGERINE JUICE
   (OR ORANGE JUICE)
→ 1 TBSP COINTREAU
→ 2 LARGE EGG WHITES
→ 4 AMARETTI BISCUITS

 MASTERCHEF TOP TIP

There is no mystery to making a hot soufflé, and it is a wonderful way to finish a meal. Make it with confidence and don't be afraid of the ingredients. The crucial thing is to whip the egg whites to the correct consistency – they should form stiff peaks. Always make sure the whisk and bowl are spotlessly clean. If you add a little lemon juice to the egg whites before whisking, it will make them stronger.
Peter Richards, Masterchef Mentor

1 Preheat the oven to 180°C/350°F/Gas Mark 4. Grease 4 ramekin dishes with the butter and dust thoroughly with caster sugar, then set aside.

2 Put the marmalade into a small saucepan with the tangerine juice and Cointreau and bring to the boil. Remove from the heat and stir to break down the marmalade. Transfer to a small saucer and leave to cool, but do not let it set.

3 Whisk the egg whites in a clean bowl until stiff. With a large metal spoon, lightly fold in the caster sugar and the cooled tangerine mixture.

4 Divide the mixture between the ramekins, leaving the rim clear. Put the dishes on a baking sheet and bake for 8 minutes, until well risen and golden brown on top. Serve immediately, with the amaretti biscuits.

Summer Berry Sabayon

If you're Italian, you will recognise the sabayon sauce as a zabaglione. The secret to getting this fluffy, delicious warm sauce right is in the whisking. You have to make sure that the mixture is whisked long enough for it to become the consistency of double cream. The addition of Frangelico is inspired, giving it a wonderful hazelnut flavour. You could use other liqueurs, such as Grand Marnier or kirsch, or marsala.

→ 4 EGG YOLKS
→ 60G (2¼OZ) CASTER SUGAR
→ 5 TBSP FRANGELICO (HAZELNUT LIQUEUR)
→ 300G (11OZ) MIXED SUMMER BERRIES, SUCH AS RASPBERRIES, STRAWBERRIES AND BLACKBERRIES
→ 2 TBSP FLAKED ALMONDS
→ MINT SPRIGS, TO DECORATE

1 Preheat the grill. Put the egg yolks and sugar in a large bowl and whisk until pale and thick, using a hand-held electric beater.

2 Add the Frangelico and place the bowl over a saucepan of gently simmering water, making sure the water doesn't touch the base of the bowl. Continue whisking for at least 10 minutes, until the mixture is pale and very foamy. It should have increased in volume dramatically.

3 Put the mixed berries into a heatproof serving dish. Spoon the sabayon over the fruit and sprinkle the almonds on top.

4 Place under a hot grill for 2–3 minutes, until the almonds and sabayon colour slightly. Decorate with sprigs of mint and serve immediately.

Inspired by contestant Caroline Brewester

Sparkling Cranberry Jellies with Orange Langue de Chat Biscuits

The key to success here is to let the mixture cool before adding the wine, so all the bubbles set with the jelly rather then being destroyed by the heat. Remember that these jellies are alcoholic and therefore should be served in little glasses.

→ 350ML (12FL OZ) GOOD-QUALITY CRANBERRY JUICE DRINK
→ 200G (7OZ) FRESH CRANBERRIES
→ 200G (7OZ) GRANULATED SUGAR
→ 6 GELATINE LEAVES
→ ABOUT ½ BOTTLE OF DRY CAVA OR OTHER DRY SPARKLING WINE
→ 4 SMALL SPRIGS OF MINT
For the biscuits:
→ GRATED ZEST OF 1 ORANGE
→ 60G (2¼OZ) UNSALTED BUTTER, SOFTENED
→ 60G (2¼OZ) CASTER SUGAR
→ 2 EGG WHITES, LIGHTLY BEATEN
→ 60G (2¼OZ) PLAIN FLOUR

1 Pour 300ml (½ pint) of the cranberry juice into a saucepan and add the cranberries and sugar. Bring to the boil, then reduce the heat and simmer for 5 minutes, until the cranberries are soft. Remove from the heat.

2 Soak the gelatine leaves in the remaining cranberry juice for 5 minutes. Meanwhile, strain the cranberries and juice through a fine sieve into a large basin, pressing the cranberries with the back of a spoon to extract all the liquid. Measure the strained liquid; you should have about 500ml (18fl oz).

3 Add the soaked gelatine to the hot liquid, stirring until dissolved. Leave to cool.

4 Make the liquid up to 900ml (1½ pints) with the Cava and stir until thoroughly combined. Let the bubbles subside, then pour into four 250ml (8fl oz) glasses. Chill until set.

5 Preheat the oven to 200°C/400°F/Gas Mark 6. For the biscuits, put the orange zest and butter into a bowl and beat well. Add the sugar and beat until pale and fluffy. Stir in the egg whites (the mixture will look slightly curdled), then beat in the flour, mixing to a fairly stiff cream.

6 Fit a piping bag with a small nozzle and fill with the mixture. Line a baking sheet with baking parchment and pipe thin strips of the mixture on to it, about 5cm (2 in) long. They will spread dramatically in the oven, so leave 5cm (2 in) between each one.

7 Bake for about 8 minutes, until they are pale gold in the centre and darker at the edges. Transfer to a wire rack to cool.

8 Serve the sparkling cranberry jellies decorated with the sprigs of mint and accompanied by the biscuits.

Avocado and Honey Ice Cream with Caramelised Aubergine

Now this is a real left-field recipe but, in the true spirit of Masterchef, Christopher wanted to push the boat out and try something different. It works surprisingly well. If you like to be innovative in your cooking, do give it a go. It might be fun not to tell people what you are serving them, to see if they can guess what it is.

→ 300ML (1/2 PINT) MILK
→ 300ML (1/2 PINT) DOUBLE CREAM
→ 6 MEDIUM EGG YOLKS
→ 175G (6OZ) CASTER SUGAR
→ 2 AVOCADOS
→ 4 TBSP RUNNY HONEY

For the caramelised aubergines:
→ 2 TBSP CLARIFIED BUTTER
→ 3 TBSP CASTER SUGAR
→ 8 SLICES OF AUBERGINE,
   CUT 8MM (1/3 IN) THICK

1 Bring the milk and cream to simmering point in a saucepan. Whisk the egg yolks and caster sugar together until pale and very thick, using a hand-held electric beater. Pour the hot (but not boiling) cream on to the egg yolk mixture, stirring vigorously until well blended.

2 Pour the mixture into a clean pan and cook over a very low heat, stirring constantly, until the custard thickens enough to coat the back of the spoon; do not let it boil. Cool the mixture down quickly by placing the pan in a sink of cold water, stirring occasionally.

3 When the custard is cold, peel and stone the avocados, then purée them in a blender or food processor with the honey. Stir into the custard, mixing well.

4 Pour the custard into an ice-cream maker and churn for 20 minutes or until it has thickened and increased in volume but not frozen completely. Pour into a container and finish in the freezer.

5 For the caramelised aubergines, melt the clarified butter in a large, non-stick frying pan over a low heat. Sprinkle half the caster sugar over the aubergine slices. Add the slices to the pan (in batches, if necessary), sugar-side down, and cook until they go a deep golden brown underneath. Sprinkle the rest of the sugar on top, then turn them over and cook until browned and tender. Serve warm, with the avocado ice cream.

List of Suppliers with Introduction by Gregg Wallace

Remember the story of the three little pigs? The lazy one built a straw house and quickly had the big bad wolf on his piggy butt. The clever one took time and built an impregnable house of brick. This is the approach everyone should take with food. You simply cannot prepare anything properly without decent materials.

My love affair with quality ingredients stems from supplying fruit and vegetables to London restaurants for over twenty years. Chefs have extremely high standards, and over the years their passion has got into my bloodstream.

Readers who have watched Masterchef will have noticed my preference for simple food. Simple does not mean easy! The simple dishes are the hardest to accomplish. Buying the best ingredients and doing as little to them as possible is, for me and many gastronomes, the ultimate in dining. Only a very confident cook will take this route, because it leaves you nowhere to hide. That simple dish must have the correct flavour and texture. The ingredients are the star turn, not the person in the funny white hat.

I love the food of Italy. In Italy, chefs seek out the best produce, then allow it to shine, unencumbered by complex sauces or vegetables carved into Mickey Mouse shapes. There is a saying, 'French food at its best shows the genius of a chef. Italian food at its best shows the genius of God.'

Everyone knocks supermarkets, but not me. They are the best dried stores I have ever seen. Nowhere else will you find such an enormous choice of biscuits, breakfast cereals, canned foods, cakes, dried foods, sweets, coffees, teas and drinks all under one roof. To give credit where it's due, we now have amazing dried goods stores conveniently located in every major town. But the problem with supermarkets is that they try to apply their hugely successful approach to dried foods to fresh ones as well, and this just doesn't work. Mother Nature simply refuses to produce animals, fish, fruit and vegetables in standard packets. Produce should be reared, hunted or grown for its flavour, not for its ability to barcode properly. Anyone who has ever grown anything, flower, fruit or vegetable, realises that no two plants ever look the same. Trust your instincts: if you see row upon row of carrots all the same size and weight, something's wrong.

Would you buy a car from someone who clearly knew nothing about them? Or a holiday from a travel agent who admitted that she had never travelled to any of the destinations? Then why are you happy to buy food from nice, polite young men and women in supermarkets who obviously know nothing about food? Ask the man behind the meat counter, the one on his way to a fancy-dress party dressed as a butcher, how long the beef has been hung. Ask the chap stacking cauliflowers on shelves his opinion of purple sprouting broccoli over calabrese. You will get hilarious responses.

Buy food from people who know their produce. Farmers' markets are an obvious example, but don't overlook ethnic shops. In my experience, Indian, Chinese, Thai, African, West Indian, Greek and Turkish shopkeepers know their stuff. They were brought up with a culture that respects food and are more than happy to share cooking tips. You can also buy from the farm. A good tip is to put the words 'meat', 'veg' and 'farm' into an Internet search engine and see what comes up – that way you'll get direct contact with the producers.

Listen, this is important! Eating is something we do every day. It's worth taking time to shop well so that we eat well. This does not have to mean buying expensive food. If we all bought seasonally we would eat tastier and cheaper foods. A strawberry may be reasonably priced on a farm in Venezuela in December, but by the time it's flown over here Club Class, had a prawn sandwich and watched the in-flight movie it's a tad more expensive.

If you want to find out more about buying and preparing good food, I recommend the following books. For a seasonal guide to fish, try *Fish* by Sophie Grigson and William Black (Headline, 1998). For meat, I would invest in *The River Cottage Meat Book* by Hugh Fearnley-Whittingstall (Hodder & Stoughton, 2004). As for vegetables, well, you'll have to wait for my veg book to be published. Or check out my farm website on www.secrettsdirect.co.uk.

LONDON

Bread and Patisserie

& Clarke's
122 Kensington Church Street,
London W8 4BH
Tel: 020 7229 2190
www.sallyclarke.com

Baker and Spice
75 Salusbury Road, London NW6 6NH
Tel: 020 7664 3636
www.bakerandspice.com

De Gustibus
53 Blandford Street, London W1H 3AF
Tel: 020 7486 6608

Euphorium Bakery
203 Upper Street, London N1 1RQ
Tel: 020 7704 6905

Konditor and Cook
10 Stoney Street, London SE1 9AD
Tel: 020 7407 5100

Lighthouse Bakery
64 Northcote Road, London SW11 6QL
Tel: 020 7228 4537
www.lighthousebakery.co.uk

Ottolenghi
287 Upper Street, London N1 2TZ
Tel: 020 7288 1454
www.ottolenghi.co.uk

Poilâne
46 Elizabeth Street, London SW1W 9PA
Tel: 020 7808 4910
www.poilane.fr

Cheese and Dairy

La Fromagerie
2-4 Moxon Street, London W1U 4EW
Tel: 020 7935 0341
www.lafromagerie.co.uk

Neal's Yard Dairy
6 Park Street, London SE1 9AB
Tel: 020 7645 3550
www.nealsyarddairy.co.uk

Paxton & Whitfield
93 Jermyn Street, London SW1Y 6JE
Tel: 020 7930 0259
www.paxtonandwhitfield.co.uk

Delicatessens and Specialist Foods

Alford's of Farringdon
506 Central Markets, Farringdon Road,
London EC1A 9NL

Arigato
48-50 Brewer Street, London W1F 9TG
Tel: 020 7287 1722

Brindisa
32 Exmouth Market, London EC1R 4QE
Tel: 020 7713 1666
www.brindisa.com

Carluccio's Caffé
Branches across the South-East
www.carluccios.com

Comptoir Gascon
63 Charterhouse Street,
London EC1M 6HJ
Tel: 020 7608 0851

Del'Aziz
24-28 Vanston Place, London SW6 1AX
Tel: 020 7386 0086

The Grocer on Elgin
6 Elgin Crescent, Notting Hill W11 2HX
Tel: 020 7221 3844
www.thegroceron.com

Jeroboams
96 Holland Park Avenue,
London W11 3RB
Tel: 020 7727 9359

Elizabeth King
34 New Kings Road, London SW6 4ST
Tel: 020 7736 2826

Megan's
571 Kings Road, London SW6 2EB
Tel: 020 7371 7837

Monte's
Canonbury Lane, London N1 2AS
Tel: 020 7354 4335

Mortimer & Bennett
33 Turnham Green Terrace,
London W4 1RG
Tel: 020 8995 4145
www.mortimerandbennett.com

Olga Stores
30 Penton Street, London N1 9PS
Tel: 020 7837 5467

Panzer's
13-19 Circus Road, London NW8 6PB
Tel: 020 7722 8596
www.panzers.co.uk

Petit Luc's Delicatessen
4 Leadenhall Market, London EC3V 1LR
Tel: 020 7283 6707

Speck
2 Holland Park Terrace,
Portland Road, London W11 4ND
Tel: 020 7229 7005
www.speck-deli.co.uk

The Spice Shop
1 Blenheim Crescent,
London W11 2EE
Tel: 020 7221 4448
www.thespiceshop.co.uk

Taj Stores
112-114 Brick Lane, London E1 6RL
Tel: 020 7377 0061

Villandry
170 Great Portland Street,
London W1W 5QB
Tel: 020 7631 3131
www.villandry.com

Fish

Chalmers & Gray
67 Notting Hill Gate, London W11 3JS
Tel: 020 7221 6177

Cope's
700 Fulham Road, London SW6 5SA
Tel: 020 7371 7300

Steve Hatt
88-90 Essex Road, London N1 8LU
Tel: 020 7226 3963

H. S. Linwood & Sons
6-7 Leadenhall Market,
London EC3V 1LR
Tel: 020 7929 0554

Food Halls

Flâneur Food Hall
41 Farringdon Road, London EC1M 3JB
Tel: 020 7404 4422

Fortnum and Mason
181 Piccadilly, London W1A 1ER
Tel: 020 7734 8040
www.fortnumandmason.com

Harrods
87–135 Brompton Road,
London SW1X 7XL
Tel: 020 7730 1234
www.harrods.com

Selfridges
400 Oxford Street, London W1A 2LR
Tel: 020 7629 1234
www.selfridges.co.uk

Fruit and Vegetables

Barbican Fruiterers and Greengrocers
26 Goswell Road, London EC1M 7AA
Tel: 020 7253 2190

Michanicou Brothers
2 Clarendon Road, London W11 3AA
Tel: 020 7727 5191

Susan's
234 Essex Road, London N1 3AP
Tel: 020 7226 6844

Meat, Poultry and Game

Allen & Co.
117 Mount Street, London W1K 3LA
Tel: 020 7499 5831

S. C. Crosby
65 Charterhouse Street,
London EC1M 6HJ
Tel: 020 7253 1239

A. Dove and Son
71 Northcote Road, London SW11 6PJ
Tel: 020 7223 5191

James Elliot
96 Essex Road, London N1 8LU
Tel: 020 7226 3658

The Ginger Pig
8–10 Moxon Street, London W1U 4EU
Tel: 020 7935 7788

Frank Godfrey
7 Highbury Park, London N5 1QJ
Tel: 020 7226 9904

A. A. King
30–34 New King Road,
London SW6 4ST
Tel: 020 7736 4004

C. Lidgate
110 Holland Park Avenue,
London W11 4UA
Tel: 020 7727 8243

Meat City
507 Central Markets,
Farringdon Road, London EC1A 9NL
Tel: 020 7253 9606

M. Moen & Sons
24 The Pavement, London SW4 0JA
Tel: 020 7622 1624

E. Wood
53 Barnsbury Street, London N1 1TP
Tel: 020 7607 1522

Wine and Spirits

La Grande Marque
55 Leadenhall Market,
London EC3V 1LT
Tel: 020 7929 3536

Lea & Sandeman
211 Kensington Church Street,
London W8 7LX
Tel: 020 7221 1982
www.londonfinewines.co.uk

Milroys of Soho
3 Greek Street, London W1V 6NX
Tel: 020 7437 9311
www.milroys.co.uk

Markets

Borough Market
8 Southwark Street, London SE1 1TL
Tel: 020 7404 1002
www.boroughmarket.org.uk

Chapel Market
Conduit Street, Grant Street and
Baron Street, London N1 9EX

North End Road Market
North End Road, London SW6 1NL
Tel: 020 8748 3020

REST OF BRITAIN AND IRELAND

*This barely scratches the surface
of the fantastic selection of suppliers
around the country, but should give
you somewhere to start! Many suppliers
offer a mail-order service.*

Bread and Patisseries

S. C. Price & Sons
7 Castle Street, Ludlow SY8 1AS
Tel: 01584 872815

Shipton Mill
Long Newnton, Tetbury GL8 8RP
Tel: 01666 505050

The Village Bakery
Melmerby, Penrith CA10 1HE
Tel: 01768 881811
www.village-bakery.com

Cheese and Dairy

The Cheese Shop
116 Northgate Street, Chester CH1 2HT
Tel: 01244 346240
www.chestercheeseshop.com

The Fine Cheese Company
29 & 31 Walcot Street, Bath BA1 5BN
Tel: 01225 448748
www.finecheese.co.uk

The House of Cheese
13 Church Street, Tetbury GL8 8JG
Tel: 01666 502865
www.houseofcheese.co.uk

I. J. Mellis
492 Great Western Road,
Glasgow G12 8EW
Tel: 0141 339 8998
www.ijmellischeesemonger.com

Delicatessens and Specialist Foods

Lewis & Cooper
92 High Street, Northallerton DL7 8PP
Tel: 01609 772880
www.lewis-and-cooper.co.uk

Provender
3 Market Square,
South Petherton TA13 5BT
Tel: 01460 240681
www.provender.net

Real Eating Company
86–87 Western Road, Hove BN3 1JB
Tel: 01273 221444
www.real-eating.co.uk

Valvona & Crolla
19 Elm Row, Edinburgh EH7 4AA
Tel: 0131 556 6066
www.valvonacrolla.co.uk

The Vineyard Delicatessen
23–24 Eld Lane, Colchester CO1 1LS
Tel: 01206 573363
www.vineyard-deli.co.uk

Fish

Fishworks
6 Green Street, Bath BA1 2JY
Tel: 01225 448707
*Branches in Bristol, Christchurch
and London*
http://www.fishworks.co.uk

John's Fish Shop Suffolk
5 East Street,
Southwold IP18 6EH
Tel: 01502 724253
www.johns-fish-shop.co.uk

Simply Organic Food Company
Horsley Road, Kingsthorpe Hollow,
Northampton NN2 6LJ
Tel: 0870 7606001
www.simplyorganic.net

Whitstable Shellfish Company
Westmead Road, Whitstable CT5 1LW
Tel: 01227 282375
www.whitstable-shellfish.co.uk

Fruit and Vegetables

Abel & Cole
www.abel-cole.co.uk

Howbarrow Organic Farm
Cartmel,
Grange-over-Sands LA11 7SS
Tel: 01539 536330
www.howbarroworganic.demon.co.uk

The Organic Farm Shop
Abbey Home Farm,
Burford Road, Cirencester GL7 5HF
Tel: 01285 640441
www.theorganicfarmshop.co.uk

Peppers by Post
Sea Spring Farm,
West Bexington, Dorchester DT2 9DD
Tel: 01308 897892
www.peppersbypost.biz

Secretts Direct
www.secrettsdirect.co.uk

Meat, Poultry and Game

Alternative Meats
Hough Farm,
Weston-under-Redcastle,
Shrewsbury SY4 5LR
Tel: 011948 840130
www.alternativemeats.co.uk

The Butts Farm Shop
South Cerney, Cirencester GL7 5QE
Tel: 01255 862224
www.buttsfarmshop.com

Kelly Turkey Farms
Springate Farm,
Bicknacre Road, Danbury CM3 4EP
Tel: 01245 223581
www.kelly-turkeys.com

Langley Chase Organic Farm
Kington Langley SN15 5PW
Tel: 01249 750 095
www.langleychase.co.uk

Swaddles Green Organic Farm
Chard TA20 3JR
Tel: 0845 456 1768
www.swaddles.co.uk

G. & R. Tudge
The Bury, Richards Castle,
Ludlow SY8 4EL
Tel: 01584 831227

D. W. Wall
14 High St, Ludlow SY8 1BS
Tel: 01584 872060

Supermarkets

Marks and Spencer
Tel: 0845 302 1234
www.marksandspencer.com

Sainsburys
Tel: 0800 636262
www.sainsburys.co.uk

Waitrose
Tel: 0800 188 884
www.waitrose.com

Wines, Beers and Spirits

Berry Bros & Rudd
Tel: 0870 900 4300
www.bbr.com

Oddbins
Tel: 0800 328 2323
www.oddbins.com

Threshers
Tel: 01707 387200
www.threshers.co.uk

Index